英汉对照名人故事

The English-Chinese Bilingual Stories of the Famous Persons

逸云‖选编

文匯出版社

目录 | Contents

II Writers and Artists 作家和艺术家 055

I 科学家和发明家
Scientists and Inventors

Morse: He Linked Every Corner of the World Up

Morse was born at Charlestown, Massachusetts, U. S. A., on the 27th April, 1791. His father was a Congregational minister of that town, and a man whose upright character and independence of mind had won for him universal respect. In no sense of the word a wealthy man, he was able, by careful economies, to send his three sons all to Yale University.

During the year 1809, Morse attended his first lecture on electricity. The subject, as taught by Day, intrigued his imagination enormously. He could think and dream of nothing but electricity. But electricity, then in its infancy, offered no possible openings for a career, so young Morse, who possessed very distinct artistic ability, decided to become a portrait painter.

Soon after his graduation from Yale, Morse met Washington Allston, then the best-known portraitist of the

United States. With Allston he came to England during 1811, returning to Boston four years later a fully equipped master of his chosen craft. Sitters were hard to find in Boston, so Morse set out on a trip through the eastern states, taking commissions for portraits on the way. During this venture he met and married, in 1818, Miss Lucretia Walker, of Concord. Until 1825 Morse flourished greatly, building up for himself a substantial reputation as an artist. Suddenly, however, his wife died, and the mainspring of his ambition was broken.

He had a family of three young children to support, so he continued painting in a desultory fashion. During 1827 his mind was again turned towards electricity by his attending a series of lectures on the subject in New York. In 1829 he journeyed once more to Europe in order to perfect himself as a painter by three years' further study.

In the autumn of 1832 he traveled home in the company of several scientists. One of them asked him in the course of conversation, "Is the velocity of electricity reduced by the length of its conducting wire?" Morse instantly recalled Benjamin Franklin's experiment, which showed that the time taken for a current to traverse several miles of wire was too minute to be measured. He thought this over for a few seconds. Then, suddenly, the whole idea of an electrical telegraph flashed into his mind.

On his return to America, Morse more or less gave up his profession in order to devote himself to the working out of his great idea. For three years he was often reduced to starvation. But fortunately he got a post in New York University. And later his colleague, Leonard Gale became his collaborator. At last, on the 2nd September, 1837, a successful experiment was made with 1,700 feet of wire, which was stretched round and round Morse's studio. In fact, the success of the trial exceeded the inventor's wildest hopes. The telegraph came into being.

After years' great efforts, lines were laid from city to city. And later the "Morse telegraph", as it was called, began to be installed in Europe. Railway companies and war departments were the first to appreciate the services offered by the telegraph.

The public regarded the invention rather suspiciously, and to the cautious, commonsense men of mid-nineteenth century industrialism anything to do with electricity seemed rather a joke than otherwise. However, a case changed their attitude unexpectedly. A particularly brutal and senseless murder was committed at Slough, and the murderer left by a train for Paddington before a hue and cry could be raised.

The Great Western Railway, however, had a telegraph line installed between Slough Station and Paddington, over which a description of the murderer was flashed, and he found the police awaiting him when the train drew into the London terminus. Without the aid of the telegraph, it is almost certain that he would have escaped. His arrest caught the popular attention, and completely broke down the great and unreasonable prejudice which had existed against the telegraph.

Unlike many other inventions, Morse reaped the rewards of his labors in the shape of a handsome fortune. For many years he continued to interest himself in telegraph enterprises, being associated with Professor Henry, among others, in gradually improving and perfecting his invention. He lived to see a telegraph line span the North American continent, and a submarine cable link America with England. Decorated and honored by many governments, universities, and public bodies, Samuel Morse died on the 2nd April, 1872.

莫尔斯：他将四海联为一体

莫尔斯于1791 年4 月27 日出生在美国马萨诸塞州的查尔斯城。他的父亲是当地的一位公理会牧师，为人正直、思想独立，周围的人都对他十分敬重。他父亲无论如何算不上富有，但凭着精打细算，把三个儿子都送进了耶鲁大学。

1809 年，莫尔斯上了他的第一堂电学课。这门由杰利米亚·戴主讲的课程大大激发了他的想象力。他白天想的、晚上梦的全是电学。但在那时，电学还处于起步阶段，提供不了什么工作机会；而年轻的莫尔斯又在艺术方面才华出众，于是他决心成为一名肖像画家。

从耶鲁毕业后不久，莫尔斯遇见了当时全美最著名的肖像画家华盛顿·阿斯顿。1811 年，他和阿斯顿一道去英格兰待了四年，返回波士顿时，他已经是一名训练有素的绘画好手了。在波士顿，人体模特很难找，于是，莫尔斯动身远行，穿越东部各州，沿途替人画像赚取佣金。1818 年，他在冒险途中遇见了来自康科德镇的卢奎西娅·沃克小姐，并与之结为夫妇。从那之后一直到1825 年，莫尔斯的事业左右逢源，建立起了作为艺术家的显赫名声。然而，他的妻子骤然离世，他一展宏图的动力也随之瓦解。

家里有三个幼子要他养活，于是他继续潦草作画。1827年，他在纽约旁听了一系列关于电学的讲座，心中重新燃起了对于电学的渴望。1829年，为了磨炼绘画技艺，他再度远赴欧洲，开始了为期三年的进修。

1832年秋季，他和几位科学家一道返回故乡。其中的一位在谈话中问他："导线的长度会使电的速度降低吗？"莫尔斯立即想到了本杰明·富兰克林的实验，实验中的电流通过了数英里长的导线，经历的时间却短暂到无法测量。他想了几秒钟，接着，心里赫然闪过了电报的想法。

回到美国之后，莫尔斯多少放弃了本职工作，专心实践起了这个伟大的想法。他在此后的三年里常常食不果腹，但终于有幸在纽约大学获得了一个职位。后来，他的同事雷纳德·盖尔与他合作，两人终于在1837年9月2日用1 700英尺的导线进行了一次成功的实验，导线围着莫尔斯的画室摆了好几周。实验的成功超出了发明者最大胆的期望，电报诞生了。

经过人们几年的辛勤努力，电报线在城市之间铺设开来。后来，人们在欧洲安装了被称为"莫尔斯电报"的装置。铁路公司和国防部门最先使用了电报。

公众对这项新发明满腹狐疑，时值19世纪中期的工业社会，在那些谨小慎微、囿于常识的人们眼中，和电有关的一切都只是笑话而已。然而，一起案件却出乎意料地改变了他们的观点。在斯劳发生了一次格外残忍、毫无意义的谋杀案,还没等人发现,杀手就已经登上火车,逃往帕丁顿。

然而,大西部铁路公司已经在斯劳和帕丁顿车站之间架设了一条电报线路,杀手的信息转眼便被传了过去。火车驶进伦敦站时,杀手发现警察已经在守株待兔了。如果不是电报的协助,罪犯多半已经逃之夭夭。他的被捕引起了公众的注意,之前对于电报毫无理由的巨大偏见也随之一扫而空。

与许多其他发明不同的是,莫尔斯的努力得到了丰厚的经济回报。多年以后,他的兴趣还保持在电报事业,他和亨利教授等人共事,逐渐提高并完善了他的这项发明。他在有生之年见证了电报线路贯通北美大陆,还目睹了海底电缆连接美洲和英格兰。许多政府、大学和公共组织对莫尔斯授予了勋章和荣誉。1872 年 4 月 2 日,塞缪尔·莫尔斯与世长辞。

(高天羽　译)

Edison: The Greatest Inventor

Thomas Alva Edison was a man of wonderful ability who had the good luck to be born at a good time. In the period just after the American Civil War the United States was growing. Conditions were right for the talents of a man like Edison.

The Edison family had come to the United States from Holland in the early part of the 18th century. Thomas Alva, the youngest of Samuel's seven children was born in 1847.

Thomas was an unusually curious child. Even at an early age he loved to read and make experiments. Because he was so dreamy and quiet, a teacher once accused him of being stupid. Thomas's mother was so displeased by this remark that she took her son out of school and never sent him back. She took charge of his education herself and taught him reading history, science and philosophy. Edison was a very quick reader and he remembered everything. Once he got the idea of starting at the first shelf of a large library and reading everything in it. But after reading through fifteen feet of books he gave up this ambition.

In order to earn money for books and for his scientific experiments, Thomas sold vegetables from the family garden. This work did not bring in enough money, so he began to sell newspapers and candy on a train that ran between Port Huron Michigan and Detroit. Because people were so eager for the latest news about the Civil War which was then at its height, Thomas decided in February 1862 when he was fifteen years old to print a newspaper of his own the *Weekly Herald,* in a baggage car of the train where he worked. In four years he earned two thousand dollars from this business.

While he worked on the train young Edison continued to experiment setting up a laboratory in the baggage car. One day a stick of phosphorus fell to the floor and set the car on fire. The conductor of the train was so angry that he threw him and all his equipment off the train at the next station; he also struck him causing a permanent injury which later made him deaf in the right ear.

One day not long after he had started his newspaper, Edison saw a child playing on the tracks in front of a train. He jumped off the station platform and snatched the child from the wheels of the train. The father who happened to be the stationmaster was so grateful that he offered to teach Edison to become a telegraph operator. He gave him lessons four days a week after the station had closed for the night and in three weeks Edison was a better telegrapher than his teacher.

Edison was sober and independent for his age, but he was restless and very careless in his dress. He began to wander from city to city and from job to job. Because his ideas were too strange to please the men who hired him, they often asked him to leave. During this time, he worked in Indianapolis, Cincinnati, Memphis, and Louisville.

Edison went to Boston where he had been promised work as a telegraph operator, mainly because of the neat handwriting in his letter of application. When he appeared in that city, he looked so untidy and strange that the superintendent asked him to return later in the day to take a test in telegraphy, with the idea of making the test so difficult that the young man could not possibly pass it. As the rapid message came in, Edison realized clerks in the station were playing a joke on him. They had arranged for the New York operator to send him a message, faster and faster, in an effort to make Edison admit that he could not write it down at such a rapid pace. But

Edison was not discouraged. He decided to outwit these fellows, and he began to send a message himself. He said to the New York operator, "Come on, don't go to sleep. Get busy!" That ended the joke, and Edison won his job, as well as the title of the fastest telegraph operator in the Western Union Company.

In 1869 he borrowed some money and went to New York. During the first three years he spent there, he nearly died of starvation. He slept in a room belonging to a company that sent information on stock prices to the business houses of New York. One day the machine that printed news about gold stopped. Six hundred banks and business houses were without information about what was being bought and sold that day. Edison succeeded in repairing the machine, and he was then offered a job as manager for $300 a month. He was soon hard at work making improvements in the machine and inventing new parts. His Universal Printer, invented at this time, printed full information about gold prices, instead of showing them only by a few letters and numbers. This was his first big success. General Marshall Lefferts, president of the Gold and Stock Telegraph Company, bought this and several other inventions of Edison's for forty thousand dollars.

Edison then put his new money to work. He opened a factory in Newark, New Jersey. Soon he had over one hundred and fifty men building machines to record stock prices, while he himself continued to work on new ideas. At one time, he had forty-five separate inventions in his laboratory, including several important improvements of the telegraph. He invented a way of sending two messages at the same time in opposite directions, and then a way of sending two messages at the same time in the same direction, in 1874 he invented and sold to Western Union a system by which four messages could be sent over one wire at the same time, two in each direction. He also perfected a new system for sending telegrams. These inventions saved Western Union millions of dollars in the cost of wires and telegraph poles alone.

Western Union then suggested to Edison that he try to develop a commercially useful telephone, Alexander Graham Bell had already patented the telephone, but Bell's telephone could be heard only over short distances. Edison added several improvements, which were adopted, and are still used in the telephone today. Western Union paid Edison one hundred thousand dollars for his inventions.

In 1876 he built a workshop and laboratory in Menlo

Park, New Jersey. He was known after that as he Wizard of Menlo Park, because of the wonderful discoveries he made there. He began to study the attempts of other men to invent an incandescent electric light. He tried over and over again to make a soft light that would be suitable for use in private houses. He tested over two thousand materials before discovering one that would work. He needed something that would become hot and give off light when electricity passed through it in a glass container from which the air had been removed. He spent a hundred thousand dollars searching for the best material. Men were sent to India, China, Brazil, and finally, Japan, where a material was finally found.

In January, 1880, the electric light was patented. Edison then built a factory for the production of his light in Menlo Park, and an electric power station in New York City. But it was fourteen years before the public really accepted the electric light. After that, the electric light business grew so greatly that Edison was able to sell his share in the electric light for more than one million dollars.

Edison patented over one thousand separate inventions during his life. He never stopped trying to learn more about science and what it could do for man. His discoveries probably increased the wealth of the world more than those of any other single man in history.

On October 18, 1931, Edison died at the age of eighty-four at his home in Orange, New Jersey. Several days later, the whole United States turned off its electric lights for one minute, in honor of the man whose discoveries had so changed and improved the life of people everywhere.

爱迪生：最伟大的发明家

托马斯·阿尔法·爱迪生是一位诞生在好时代里的天才人物。南北战争以后，美国正在成长壮大，各种条件对于像爱迪生这样的天才都是有利的。

爱迪生家族在 18 世纪早期从荷兰来到美国。托马斯·阿尔法生于 1847 年，是塞缪尔的七个孩子中最小的一个。

托马斯是一个好奇心特强的孩子。即使还在幼年时代，他就爱读书和做实验。因为他如此爱好空想和不声不响，以致一位老师有一次骂他愚蠢。托马斯的母亲对这个评语很不高兴，她把孩子从学校接回来再也没送他回去过。母亲自己教育孩子，教他阅读历史、科学和哲学书籍。爱迪生读起书来，领会得快，而且过目不忘。有一次他异想天开，要从一所大图书馆的第一个书架看起，看完书架上每一本书。但在看完了一些15英尺厚的书后，他放弃了这个野心。

为了挣钱买书和搞科学实验，托马斯就去卖他家菜园中的蔬菜。这工作挣不到足够的钱，所以他就开始在密歇根州一列专跑休伦港和底特律的火车上卖报纸和糖果。因为人们在南北战争的高潮中急于了解战争的最新情况，托马斯在1862年2月间，在他15岁时，决定在他所工作的火车行李厢上印刷他自己的报纸《先驱周报》。四年之间他通过这份报纸赚了2 000美元。

年轻的爱迪生在火车上工作时继续搞实验，在行李厢上建立了一间实验室。有一天，一根磷棒掉在地板上使这节车厢着火。列车长十分生气，在下一个车站把他和他的所有实验设备都扔下了火车，还揍了他一顿，造成永久性伤害，使爱迪生右耳聋了。

爱迪生在开办他的报纸后不久，有一天火车进站时他看见一个小孩在铁轨上玩耍。他急忙从站台上跳下把小孩从火车轮子下抢救出来。这孩子的父亲正好是站长，他很感激，主动提出要教会爱迪生成为电报员。他在车站夜晚关门后，每周给爱迪生上四次课，三个星期之后爱迪生便成为比他老师更好的电报员了。

就他的年龄来说，爱迪生很稳重，有独立性，但他很不安定，而且对于衣着很不注意。他开始从一个城市漫游到另一个城市，从一个职业换到另一个职业。因为他的想法太离奇，不能使雇用他的人满意，雇主们常常叫他卷起铺盖走人。在这段时间里，他在印第安纳波利斯、辛辛那提、孟菲斯和路易斯维尔等城市工作过。

爱迪生到了波士顿，在那里有人答应给他电报员的工作，主要因为他的求职信中字迹写得工整。当他在波士顿露面时，他是如此的衣冠不整，怪里怪气，以致主管人叫他当天晚些时候去参加电报技术的考试，目的是要故意出难题，使这位青年考试不及格。当电报迅速拍进来时，爱迪生意识到电报局的职工们是在和他开玩笑。他们已经和纽约市的电报员安排好，给爱迪生拍一份电报来，越拍越快，企图迫使爱迪生承认他抄不下这么快的电报。但爱迪生没有泄气。他决心以智取胜，于是他开始自己拍出一份电报。他对纽约市的电报员说："来吧，别去睡觉，使劲吧！"这就结束了这场玩笑，爱迪生也赢得了他的职位，同时还赢得了西联电讯公司最快电报员的称号。

1869 年爱迪生借了些钱去了纽约，他在纽约的头三年里，几乎快被饿死。他睡在一家公司的一间房子里，这公司专给纽约各商行提供股票行情。一天，那台印刷黄金行情的机器不动了。六百家银行和商行都收不到关于那天买卖的商情，爱迪生把这机器修好了，因此公司给了他一个经理的职位，月薪 300 美元。他很快就努力改进这台机器，并且还发明了许多新部件。他当时发明的万能印刷机印出了关于金价的全部情报，而不只是以少数字母和数字来显示行情。这是他第一个巨大的成功，金价和股票电报公司的经理马歇尔·莱费兹将军出资四万美元把这台机器和爱迪生的其他几项发明买了下来。

爱迪生就拿这新到手的钱做生意。他在新泽西州纽华克市开了一家工厂。不久后，他就雇了一百五十人制造记录股票行情的机器，而他自己则继续试验他的一些新想法。有一段时间在他实验室里共有四十五个不同的发明项目，包括几项对于电报机的重要改进。他想出了一种方法，可从两个相反方向同时各拍出一份电报，随后又想出一种方法，可从一个方向同时拍两份电报。1874 年他发明并卖给西联电讯公司一种装置，可以在一根电线上拍发四份电报，即从每一方向可同时拍发两份电报。他还改进了拍电报的系统，使之趋于完美。这些发明，仅在电线和电线杆的成本上就为西联电讯公司节约了几百万美元。

西联电讯公司又向爱迪生建议：叫他试制一部商用电话，亚历山大·贝尔已经取得了电话机的专利，但贝尔的电话机只能在短距离内接听。爱迪生作了几项改进，这些改进，直到今天仍然应用在电话上。西联电讯公司为此几项发明付给爱迪生 10 万美元。

1876年，爱迪生在新泽西州门罗园建造了一个车间和实验室，由于他在那里搞出了许多奇妙的发明，以后他被人们称为“门罗园的巫师”。他开始研究别人为发明白热电灯所作的尝试。他一次又一次地试制一种适合家用的柔光灯。在找到这种适合的材料之前，他竟试验了两千多种材料。他需要某种可放在抽去空气的玻璃容器内、通过电流后能变热并发出光来的材料。他花了10万美元寻找最好的材料。他派人去印度、中国、巴西，最后终于在日本找到了。

在1880年1月，他取得了电灯专利权。爱迪生在门罗园建造了一家生产电灯的工厂，并在纽约市建成了一座发电站。但是14年后，人们才真正接受他的电灯。从那以后，电灯业发展得规模如此之大，以致爱迪生出售他的电灯股票时，竟得了一百多万美元。

爱迪生一生中拥有一千多种发明专利，为了学习更多的科学并使科学为人类服务，他永不停歇。他的各种发明为世界增加的财富可能比历史上任何一个人都多。

1931年10月18日，爱迪生在新泽西州奥伦奇城的家中去世，享年84岁。几天后全美国都停电一分钟以纪念这个以他的发明大大改变并改善了各地人民生活的人。

Where Are We From?
Darwin Told Us the Answer

Like Spencer and like Huxley, Darwin was obliged to become a famous man of science contrary to both the wishes of his family and his own expectation. His father sent him to a grammar school, where he acknowledged that he did not learn anything. He was considered to be a stupid boy, with a dirty habit of collecting insects and putting them in boxes — beetles, worms, and other creeping things which disgusted his teacher.

Darwin was sent to the Edinburgh University, with his father's strict orders to study medicine, and to stop collecting spiders, beetles, etc. He tried very hard to obey; but the sight of blood made him sick, and he could not bear the dissecting room. He therefore at last notified his father that it was simply impossible for him ever to become a doctor. Therefore his father ordered him to become a clergyman. This project met with an obstacle of quite an unexpected kind. The lad was as truthful as he was tender-hearted; and he felt obliged to report that, after an examination of the dogmas, he could not quite conscientiously become a clergyman.

He was subsequently sent to Cambridge. He was always, even in the grounds of the university, hunting for curious insects; and there is a funny story about one of his adventures in this line. One day upon an old tree he saw three beetles each of a kind which he had never seen before. He caught one in his left hand and one in his right hand — thus he had both hands occupied; but the third beetle was running away very fast. In his anxiety to catch it, he put the beetle which he held in his right hand into his mouth, so as to have that hand free. But the beetle immediately squirted into his mouth some acrid secretion that burnt his tongue horribly, so that he was obliged to spit it out; and the two beetles escaped. This is a very good instance of the recklessness of enthusiasm.

He passed through Cambridge in the ordinary way, not showing any great brilliancy in the regular course of studies, but endearing himself to his friends and always continuing his researches in natural history.

It was then that one of his fellow students obtained for him opportunity that was to make him famous. The English

Government was sending that ship Beagle on an exploring expedition to South America, and a naturalist was wanted to accompany the expedition. Darwin was recommended by his university friend, and was given the chance after some hesitation.

The cause of the hesitation was a very curious one. The commander of the ship had studied the old false science of Lavater; and he observed that Darwin had a small flat nose. He thought that nobody having a small flat nose could possess enough energy and determination to do the work required for the Beagle expedition. How much he was mistaken, the world now knows. Of all scientific workers of the 19th century, there is certainly not one who labored more incessantly, and who achieved a greater amount of work than Charles Darwin. The events of the voyage are related in the most delightful book of travel ever written in English.

Thousands who have heard of Darwin's discovery do not know how that discovery happened to be made. It was made, or rather suggested, by the reading of the book of Malthus, *On Population*. Malthus had long before Darwin proclaimed the existence of that law of struggle for existence between species, which prevents the earth from ever becoming populous beyond a certain limit. Remembering certain observations which he had made in South America and elsewhere, it occurred to Darwin that the existence of the ten millions of different species of animals and plants known to exist could be explained according to the survival of the fittest types in that struggle announced by Malthus. This led to the origin of the great book. But remember that only a man of enormous practical knowledge could have seen in this way to thus profit by the reading of Malthus.

我们从何而来？达尔文给出了答案

像斯宾塞和赫胥黎一样，达尔文也是不得以才成为科学名人的，这既非他自己的愿望，又有违家人的期许。他父亲最初将他送进语法学校就读，他后来承认自己什么都没学到。师长认为他是个愚蠢的男孩，有用盒子收集昆虫的肮脏习惯——他的藏品包括甲虫、蠕虫和其他令师长大倒胃口的爬行生物。

父亲接着把他送进爱丁堡大学，并责令他主攻医学，不准再收集蜘蛛和甲虫。他努力遵从父命，但是鲜血令他晕头转向，解剖室也令他难以忍受。他于是知会父亲，说自己根本无法成为医生。父亲于是下令,命他当一名教士。这个计划却遇到了未曾预料的障碍。小伙子不仅心肠软,还是个老实人;他觉得应该如实告诉父亲:他在查看教义之后,发现自己无法真心诚意地做一名教士。

接着,他又被送到剑桥大学就读。他整天抓捕奇异的昆虫,即便在大学校园里也从不间断,关于他的这个嗜好,有一个冒险故事讲得颇有趣味:一天,他在一棵老树上见到了三只甲虫,它们分属不同的类别,都是他以前没有见过的。他伸出左手抓了一只,又伸出右手抓了一只 —— 这样一来,两只手就都装满了;但就在这时,第三只甲虫趁机快速逃跑。情急之下,达尔文把右手里的甲虫塞进嘴里,好腾出一只空手抓住第三只。但在他嘴里的那只甲虫立即喷出了几滴辛辣的分泌物,他的舌头严重灼伤,只得将甲虫一口吐出,另两只甲虫见状溜之大吉。这个例子很好地显示了达尔文的无畏热情。

他平淡无奇地念完了剑桥的学业,在常规课程中并没有显示出多大的聪慧,和朋友们倒是过从甚密,研究起自然史来也是孜孜不倦。

就在这时,他的一位同学为他找了个令他日后成名的机会。英国政府正要将猎兔犬号派往南美进行勘测,途中正需要携带一名博物学家。达尔文获得了大学友人的推荐,当局在犹豫一阵之后给了他这个机会。

犹豫的原因十分奇怪。船上的指挥官对拉瓦特陈腐的伪科学理论做过一番研究;他观察到达尔文的鼻子又扁又小。而他觉得鼻子小而扁平者势必缺乏精力和决心,无法胜任远征中需要完成的工作。现在,人们明白了他的错误有多么离谱。在19世纪的科学工作者中,根本没有人像达尔文那样终日辛劳,也没人取得了像他那么大的成就。达尔文把这次远航中的事件记录下来,成就了以英语书写的游记中最令人愉悦的一本。

许多人听说过达尔文的发现,但其中有数以千计并不知道它的由来。达尔文能有这项发现,是因为读了马尔萨斯的著作《人口论》;也可以说,他的发现是受了马尔萨斯的启发。早在达尔文之前,马尔萨斯就曾宣扬不同物种之间存在竞争的法则,他认为,正是这条法则才让地球上的生物总数不会超过某个限度。回忆起自己在南美和其他各地的发现,达尔文想到了这一点:地球上的动植物种类成千上万、形态各异,其原因恰好可以用马尔萨斯宣称的“物竞天择,适者生存”这一法则予以解释。他的那本伟大著作即发端于此。但是不要忘记一点:只有掌握大量实用知识的人,才能从马尔萨斯的著作中获得教益。

（高天羽　译）

Einstein: Person of Century

Albert Einstein was born in the small town of Ulm, Germany, and grew up in the suburbs of Munich, where his father owned a small electrical factory. As a youngster, he showed very few signs that he would one day be called a scientific genius. He was very slow in learning to talk. He did so poorly at school that his teachers called him "dull and backward". That was one time the teachers were wrong.

Actually, Albert Einstein was extremely intelligent. By the age of 12 he had taught himself geometry and calculus —— two difficult subjects usually taught in high school and college.

Einstein was fond of children, and often he would help a little neighbor girl do her arithmetic homework. The famous professor lived a quiet life. In the evenings he enjoyed chatting with friends or playing his violin.

In 1905, however, he was to publish a theory which stands as one of the most complicated examples of human imagination in history. His "*Theory of Relativity*" had a profound and surprising influence on society and culture. Einstein earned the Nobel Prize for Physics in 1921 for his work. In 1939, six years after he fled European fascism and settled at Princeton University, Einstein, a pacifist, signed a letter to President Roosevelt urging the United States to develop an atomic bomb before Nazi Germany did. Roosevelt took the advice and formed the "Manhattan Project" that secretly developed the first atomic weapon.

He deeply loved U. S. A., where he had found peace and freedom, and in 1940 he became an American citizen. Einstein died in 1955 at the age of 76. He will long be remembered as a gentle, modest man whose scientific genius opened up a whole new world of knowledge. His name will go down in history as one of the greatest thinkers who ever lived.

爱因斯坦：世纪伟人

阿尔伯特·爱因斯坦出生于德国的小镇乌尔姆。他在慕尼黑市郊长大，他的父亲在那里拥有一家小型电厂。小的时候，他并没有显示出将来会成为科学天才的任何迹象。他在学习说话这方面,进步缓慢。在学校,他的表现欠佳,因此,老师说他“迟钝或滞后”。对这件事,老师犯了个错误。

事实上,阿尔伯特·爱因斯坦是相当聪明的。他 12 岁的时候就自学几何和微积分 —— 这在高中甚至大学都是很难的学科。

爱因斯坦喜欢小孩儿,他常常帮助邻家的小女孩儿做算术作业。这位著名的科学家一生过着平静的生活。晚上,他喜欢和朋友聊天或拉小提琴。

1905 年,他发表了他的理论,这个理论至今仍然是人类想象力最复杂的典范之一。他的“相对论”对社会和文化都产生了深远的和惊人的影响。由于他的贡献,他获得了 1921 年的诺贝尔物理学奖。1939 年,也就是在他逃脱欧洲法西斯主义的控制来到普林斯顿大学之后的第六年,作为和平主义者的爱因斯坦致信当时的罗斯福总统要求美国赶在纳粹德国之前研制出原子弹。罗斯福采纳了他的建议,制定了“曼哈顿计划”,秘密地研制出第一个核武器。

他深爱着美国,因为那里有和平和自由。1940 年,他成为美国的公民。1955 年,他去世了,享年 76 岁。他在人们心目中永远是温和、谦虚的人,他在科学方面的天赋为人类开创了崭新的知识世界。作为有史以来最伟大的思想家之一,他的名字将永远载入史册。

Hubble: He Saw a Vast Universe beyond the Milky Way

Hubble majored in science as an undergraduate at the University of Chicago. A tall powerfully built young man, he excelled at basketball and boxing (fight promoters reportedly tried to talk him into turning pro). In England, Hubble kept up his muscular pursuits: he fought, ran track and played on one of the first baseball teams ever organized in the British Isles.

His official academic focus shifted, thanks to a promise made to his dying father that he would study law rather than science. On his return to America, he took a position as a high school Spanish teacher.

After a year, he signed on as a graduate student at Yerkes Observatory in Wisconsin and embarked on the work that would one day make him famous: studying nebulae (from the Latin word for cloud).

Hubble's skills as an astronomer were impressive enough

to earn him an offer from the prestigious Mount Wilson Observatory. World War I kept him from accepting right away, but in 1919 Hubble arrived at observatory headquarters, ready to start observing with the just completed 100 - inch Hooker Telescope, the most powerful on earth.

Up on the mountain, Hubble encountered his greatest scientific rival, Harlow Shapley, who had already made his reputation by measuring the size of the Milky Way. Shapley claimed that the Milky Way was the whole cosmic ball of wax. The luminous nebulae were, he insisted, clouds of glowing gas that were relatively nearby.

Hubble wasn't so sure. And in 1924, three years after Shapiey departed to take over the Harvard Observatory, Hubble found proof to the contrary. He saw a vast universe beyond the Milky Way, then found the first hints that it began with a Big Bang.

Hubble's scientific reputation was made almost overnight by his discovery that the universe is vast and the Milky Way insignificant. But he had already moved on to a new problem. For years, astronomers had noted that light from the nebulae was redder than it should be. The most likely cause of this so-called red shifting was motion away from the observer. (The same sort of thing happens with sound: a police car's siren seems to drop in pitch abruptly as the car races past a listener.)

Hubble and his assistant began measuring the distance to these receding nebulae and found what is now known as Hubble's Law: the farther away a galaxy is from Earth, the faster it's racing away. Could it be that the universe as a whole is rapidly expanding? The conclusion was extraordinary, almost mind-blowing, yet seemed inescapable.

In 1931, during a visit to Caltech, Einstein, the great physicist, traveled to the top of Mount Wilson to see the telescope and thank Hubble personally for delivering him from folly.

Hubble's last great contribution to astronomy was a central role in the design and construction of the Hale Telescope on Palomar Mountain. Four times as powerful as the Hooker, the Hale would be the largest telescope on Earth for four decades. It would have been even longer, but its completion was interrupted by World War Ⅱ.

Hubble finally got his hands on the Hale when it went into service in 1949. It was too late: he had suffered a major heart attack, and he never fully regained the stamina it took to spend all night in a freezing-cold observatory. No imaginable discovery, however, could have added to his reputation.

Hubble's astronomical triumphs earned him worldwide scientific honor and made him the toast of Hollywood during the 1930s and 1940s — the confidant of Aldous Huxley and a friend to Charlie Chaplin, Helen Hayes and William Randolph Hearst.

The only recognition that eluded him was a Noble Prize — and not for lack of effort on his part. He tried everything. In the late 1940s he even hired a publicity agent to promote his cause. Alas, there was no prize for astronomy, and by the time Nobel committee decided astronomy could be viewed as a branch of physics, it was too late. Insiders say Hubble was on the verge of winning when he died in 1953.

Hubble would have been consoled by the fact that his name adorns the Hubble Space Telescope, which probes the cosmos to depth he could not have imagined but would have fully appreciated. Whatever marvels the Hubble Telescope reveals, they are all played out on the stage Edwin Hubble first glimpsed from a lonely mountaintop in California.

哈勃：他的目光越过银河，看见了一片浩瀚的宇宙

哈勃在芝加哥大学念本科时主修理科。他是个高大壮实的青年男子，擅长篮球和拳击（据说，拳击赞助商曾劝说他改行做职业拳手）。到了英国之后，哈勃继续从事那些力量型的运动：他格斗，赛跑，还参加过英伦三岛最早的棒球队之一。

他的求学之路曾中途转向，因为父亲临终时他曾保证，自己会修读法律，而非科学。回到美国之后，他在中学里教授西班牙语。

一年之后，他受雇威斯康星的叶凯士天文台，在那里攻读研究生，并开始从事日后使他闻名的工作：研究星云（nebulae 在拉丁文里意为“云”）。

哈勃是位才华出众的天文学家，也因此获得了在威尔逊天文台工作的机会。时值第一次世界大战，他未能立即上任，但他还是在1919年来到了天文台总部，开始用刚刚完工的胡克望远镜观察天体。胡克望远镜直径100英寸，是当时世界上功能最强的天文望远镜。

哈勃在山上遇见了科研上的最大对手，哈罗·沙普

利，后者当时已经凭借对银河系大小的测量确立了名声。他宣称，宇宙中就只有银河系而已；并坚持认为，那些闪光的星云不过是离地球较近的发光气体组成的云雾。

对此，哈勃却将信将疑。1924 年，就在沙普利离开威尔逊天文台，前去执掌哈佛天文台后的第三年，哈勃找到了相反的证据。他的目光越过银河，看见了一片浩瀚的宇宙，接下来，他又首度发现了宇宙源于大爆炸的蛛丝马迹。

发现了宇宙的浩瀚和银河系的渺小之后，哈勃在科学界一夜成名。但那时的他已经在研究新的问题了。天文学家多年来一直注意到一个现象：星云发出的光的颜色要比理论上更红。这种“红移”现象最可能的原因是发光物体正在远离观察者。（声音方面也有类似的现象：警车驶过之后，警铃的音调会骤然降低。）

哈勃和他的助手开始测量起了那些远离的星云到地球的距离，并发现了现在被称为“哈勃定律”的现象：星系距离地球越远，其远离地球的速度就越快。那么，整个宇宙会不会都在快速扩张呢？结论异乎寻常，几乎令人震惊，但似乎又无可避免。

1931 年，大物理学家爱因斯坦来到加州理工学院访问，他登上威尔逊山的顶峰，参观了望远镜，并亲自感谢哈勃把他从愚蠢的想法中挽救了出来。

哈勃对天文学最后的杰出贡献,就是主持设计和建造了位于帕洛马尔山上的海尔望远镜。海尔望远镜的威力是胡克的四倍,在建成后的四十年里一直是世界上最大的天文望远镜。这段时间原本可以更长,但第二次世界大战使它未能如期完工。

海尔望远镜于 1949 年开始服役,哈勃终于能够亲手操作它了。但时间已经太晚:他发作了一次严重的心脏病,从此再也没能恢复在寒冷刺骨的天文台里工作整晚的精力。但在这时,他的名声已经如日中天,即使再有发现,也无法更进一步了。

哈勃在天文学领域的成功为他在国际科学界赢得了声誉,也使他在三四十年代成了好莱坞的红人 —— 他和阿道斯·赫胥黎成了知己,和查理·卓别林、海伦·海斯,以及威廉·兰道夫·赫斯特都交上了朋友。

他唯一缺乏的认可是一尊诺贝尔奖 —— 倒不是他本人未曾努力。他试过一切办法,甚至在 40 年代晚期雇了一名公关经纪人来鼓吹自己的事业。可叹的是,诺贝尔奖中没有设立天文学的奖项。而等到诺贝尔评奖委员会决定将天文学视作物理学的分支时,为时已晚。据内部人士透露,哈勃在 1953 年去世时,就快要得奖了。

哈勃如果泉下有知,一定会觉得宽慰,因为哈勃太空望远镜就是以他的名字命名的。这台望远镜对宇宙进行了深度探索，那种深度，他虽然无从想象，但完全能够理解。无论哈勃望远镜呈现了什么样的好戏，其上演之处，都是埃德温·哈勃在加州的孤山之巅瞥见的舞台。

（高天羽　译）

Hilleman: The Man Who Saved People's Life

Maurice R. Hilleman, the vaccine developer who may have saved more lives than any other scientist of the 20th century, died from cancer at Chestnut Hill Hospital in Philadelphia. He was 85.

In a remarkably productive career, Hilleman and his team created more than 40 human and animal vaccines, including those for measles, mumps, chickenpox, rubella, hepatitis A and B, and meningitis.

His team at Merck & Co. developed eight of the 14 vaccines that are routinely given to young children in this country. Those vaccines effectively banished many of the most disabling and deadly childhood diseases in the United States and the rest of the world.

Hilleman was also the first to identify how the influenza virus mutates, and he virtually single handedly spearheaded creation of the vaccine that prevented the Asian flu outbreak of 1957 from becoming a repeat of the 1918 Spanish flu pandemic, which killed 20 million people worldwide.

He played key roles in the discovery of the cold-producing adeno viruses, the hepatitis viruses and the cancer-causing virus SV－40, among others. He was also the first to produce a vaccine against a virally induced cancer.

In later life, Hilleman was an advisor to the World Health Organization, the US National Vaccine Program and other groups, traveling throughout the world to promote vaccination.

He never won a Nobel Prize, because those awards are designed to honor basic research, not practical applications. But Hilleman received many other awards, including the 1988 National Medal of Science, the nation's highest honor, which was presented by President Reagan.

That was a long distance to travel for a boy born on a high-plains farm near Miles City in eastern Montana.

Maurice and his seven older siblings were raised by relatives on a farm not far from the Little Bighorn battlefield 100 miles southwest of his birthplace. They tended cattle and chickens, raised vegetables and made brooms that they sold in town.

The future scientist took a special interest in the chickens, caring for them, learning about them, even figuring out how to hypnotize roosters. That experience proved invaluable in later years, because many of his creations were produced in chicken eggs.

When he graduated from Custer County High School in 1937, there was no money for college, and Hilleman took a job at the local J. C. Penney store, intending to make a career with the company. But when his oldest brother came home from seminary that summer, he demanded that Maurice go to college.

The future vaccine developer got a scholarship to what is now Montana State University in Bozeman and then a fellowship to the University of Chicago for graduate study. His prize-winning thesis reported the first way to identify different strains of chlamydia, one of the microorganisms that cause venereal disease.

He achieved this feat, which many at the time believed impossible, by using antibodies produced when he injected chlamydia from parrots into chickens.

His first job was at E. R. Squibb & Sons, where he developed his first vaccine, which protected American troops from the Japanese B encephalitis virus while fighting in the Pacific during World War Ⅱ.

In 1948, Hilleman went to Walter Reed Army Medical Center in Washington, D. C., where he began research on the influenza virus. He showed that the virus underwent two major forms of mutation, called drift and shift.

Drift is the slow, subtle change in surface characteristics that necessitates the production of a new vaccine each year. Shift is a major change in those characteristics that produces, in effect, an entirely new virus to which the population has no resistance. A shift triggered the 1918 pandemic.

Hilleman was reading the *New York Times* in his basement office at Walter Reed on April 17, 1957, when he saw an article about a flu outbreak in Hong Kong that had already afflicted 250,000 people. He was struck by a reference to "glassy-eyed children", which suggested high fevers.

In his usual earthy manner, he recalled later, "I said, son of a bitch. This is pandemic flu."

He ordered US Army researchers to collect throat swabs from some of the Hong Kong victims, and his team worked nine days, 14-hour a day to isolate the virus, which he showed to be a new strain of influenza. Blood samples from the US public showed no resistance to the virus, indicating that it had the potential to cause deaths on a large scale.

Hilleman notified public health authorities about the danger and provided samples of the virus to vaccine manufacturers.

He also insisted that chicken breeders spare the lives of roosters that otherwise would have been slaughtered, allowing them to fertilize the 40 million eggs that were used to prepare the new vaccine.

As a result of his efforts, the US death toll was held to 69,000, only about double the normal toll during flu season.

Later that year, Hilleman joined Merck. His first project for Merck was one of his few failures. His team developed one of the first polio vaccines, but Hilleman discovered that the monkey cells used to grow the weakened polio virus for the vaccine also contained another virus, SV-40, that produced cancer in animals.

Although Hilleman showed that SV-40 did not harm people, Merck withdrew the vaccine.

The company's faith in him was soon rewarded, however, when he developed the first practical measles vaccine, which used an attenuated virus grown in chicken embryos. But

Hilleman soon found that the embryos also contained a chicken virus that caused leukemia.

To make his vaccine, he turned to Kimber Farms, a Northern California poultry operation that was breeding leukemia-free chickens. The company didn't want to part with its prized specimens, but Hilleman discovered that Kimber's research director was a fellow Montanan. He got his birds.

"Montana blood runs very thick," he said later, "and chicken blood runs even thicker with me."

Epidemiologists estimate that the measles vaccine has saved one million lives annually over the 40 years since its development, and measles has been eradicated from the globe.

Hilleman's work on the mumps virus was triggered when he came home one evening and found that his daughter Jeryl Lynn, then 5, was in the early stages of the illness. He rushed to his lab to collect swabs and culture media, swabbed her mouth, and placed the swab in beef broth in the freezer to await his return from a business trip the next morning.

When he got home, he isolated the Jeryl Lynn strain of the mumps virus and produced the first vaccine against it.

Hilleman overcame immunological problems to combine several vaccines into single shots, such as the well-known

MMR vaccine for measles, mumps and rubella. He also developed a vaccine for hepatitis B, which is one of the primary causes of liver cancer — the first vaccine to protect against cancer.

Hilleman recently reflected on his work when an endowed chair in his name was established at Children's Hospital or Philadelphia:

"Looking back on one's lifetime, you say, Gee, what have I done? Have I done enough for the world to justify having been here? That's a big worry — to people from Montana, at least."

"And I would say I'm kind of pleased about all this," he added. "I'm not smug about it, but I'm pleased I devoted seven days a week. And I would do it all over again, because there's great joy in being useful, and that's the satisfaction you get out of it. Other than that, it's the quest of science and winning a battle over these bugs."

希勒曼：挽救人类生命的人

莫里斯·R. 希勒曼因患癌症在费城栗山医院去世，享年85岁。作为一位疫苗研制者，他挽救的生命可能比20世纪的任何一位科学家都要多。

在成就斐然的职业生涯中，希勒曼和他的研究小组研制出40多种人类和动物疫苗，其中包括麻疹疫苗、腮腺炎疫苗、水痘疫苗、风疹疫苗、甲肝和乙肝疫苗以及脑膜炎疫苗。

美国儿童通常接种的14种疫苗中有8种是他在默克制药公司的研究小组研制出来的。这些疫苗在美国和世界其他地方有效地消灭了许多令儿童致残和致死的疾病。

希勒曼也是确认流感病毒是如何变异的第一人。事实上，他独自一人率先研制出流感疫苗，从而避免了1957年爆发的亚洲流感造成和1918年西班牙流感疫情同样的危害，而在1918年的疫情中全世界失去2 000万人。

对于导致感冒的腺病毒、肝炎病毒和致癌的SV－40病毒以及其他病毒的发现，他起到了关键作用。他还第一个研制出用于预防由病毒引起的癌症的疫苗。

晚年，他担任了世界卫生组织、美国国家疫苗项目和其他组织的顾问，到世界各地去宣传接种疫苗。

他从没有获得过诺贝尔奖，因为诺贝尔奖旨在奖励基础研究而非实际应用。但希勒曼获得了不少其他奖项，包括1988年里根总统颁发的全国科学奖章，这是美国最高的荣誉。

对一个出生于蒙大拿东部迈尔斯城附近高原农场的男孩来说，走到这一步经历了漫漫长途。

莫里斯和七个哥哥姐姐都是亲戚一手带大的，他家的亲戚住在离小比格霍恩战场不远的一个农场上，小比格霍恩战场就位于他的出生地西南100英里处。他们养牛、养鸡、种蔬菜、制作扫帚并拿到镇上出售。

这个未来的科学家对鸡特别感兴趣，他照料鸡群、了解鸡群，甚至琢磨如何给公鸡催眠。日后证明这段经历对他极为可贵，因为他的很多发明创造都是在鸡蛋里搞出来的。

1937年希勒曼从卡斯特县立中学毕业，当时没有钱上大学，于是他在彭尼公司当地的连锁店里找了份工作，准备在这家公司里干一番事业。但是那年夏天他的大哥从神学院回来，他要求莫里斯上大学。

这位未来的疫苗研制者获得了位于博兹曼的蒙大拿州立大学的奖学金，接着又得到了进入芝加哥大学攻读研究生的奖学金。他的获奖论文首次提出了甄别不同菌株衣原体的办法。衣原体是导致性病的微生物中的一种。

他的这项成果是通过将鹦鹉身上的衣原体注入鸡身上然后利用其产生的抗体取得的，当时很多人认为这一成就是不可能的事。

他在施贵宝父子公司得到了第一份工作，在该公司他研制出自己的第一个疫苗，这种疫苗保证了二战期间在太平洋作战的美军免于感染日本乙型脑炎病毒。

1948年，希勒曼到华盛顿特区的沃尔特·里德陆军医疗中心工作，在那里他开始研究流感病毒。他证明流感病毒呈现出两种主要的变异形式，称为微变和巨变。

微变就是表面特征发生缓慢、细微的变化，使得每年生产新的疫苗成为必要。巨变就是其特征发生重大变化，实际上是产生一种全新的病毒，人类对该种新病毒没有抵抗力。正是一次巨变引起了1918年的流感大流行。

1957年4月17日，希勒曼在沃尔特·里德陆军医疗中心的地下室办公室翻阅《纽约时报》时，看到一篇文章说中国香港爆发了流感，已经有25万人染病。文中提到的“目光呆滞的儿童”引起了他的关注，这表明孩子在发高烧。他后来以其一贯率直的方式回忆说：“我当时说道，‘狗娘养的，这是流行性感冒。’”

他指示美国陆军研究人员收集用拭子取下的中国香港一些流感患者的咽喉化验标本，而他的研究小组每天工作14个小时，用了9天时间分离出了病毒。他证明这是一种新型的流感病毒。美国公众的血样表明对这种病毒没有抵抗力，这预示它可能会导致人类大量死亡。

希勒曼向公共卫生当局报告了其危险性，并向疫苗生产商提供了病毒样本。

他还坚决要求养鸡人不要宰杀公鸡，让它们使4 000万枚鸡蛋受精，然后用这些鸡蛋来研制新疫苗。

在他的努力下，美国流感死亡人数控制在6.9万人，仅比流感爆发季节的正常死亡人数多出一倍。

当年年末,希勒曼加盟默克公司。为默克公司做的第一个项目是他为数不多的几次失败之一。他的研究小组研制了第一批脊髓灰质炎疫苗,但是希勒曼发现用来将弱化脊髓灰质炎病毒培育成疫苗的猴子细胞还带有另一种病毒 SV－40,这种病毒在动物身上致癌。

尽管希勒曼证明 SV－40 对人无害,但是默克公司还是收回了这种疫苗。

然而,该公司对他的信任很快得到了回报,他研制出第一种实用的麻疹疫苗,这种疫苗使用的是在鸡胚胎中培养的减毒病毒。但是希勒曼不久发现这种胚胎也含有一种能够导致白血病的鸡病毒。

为了研制疫苗,他求助北加州的养禽企业金伯农场,那里饲养着没有白血病的鸡。这家养鸡公司不愿意把自己的珍贵鸡种卖掉,但是希勒曼发现金伯农场的研究主管是蒙大拿老乡。他终于如愿以偿了。

他后来说:“蒙大拿乡情浓,对我来说鸡情更浓。”

流行病学家估计,麻疹疫苗开发后的 40 多年中,每年挽救了 100 万人的生命,现在麻疹已在全球灭绝。

希勒曼研究腮腺炎病毒的起因是,一天晚上他回到家,发现当时只有 5 岁的女儿杰瑞尔・林恩正处在腮腺炎发病初期。他急忙跑到实验室拿来药签和培养基,用药签擦了一下她的嘴，然后将取样药签放在冰箱里的牛肉汤里，等第二天上午出差回来再着手研究。

回来后，他分离出了杰瑞尔·林恩感染的腮腺炎病毒，并研制出第一个对付这种病毒的疫苗。

希勒曼攻克了免疫学难题，将好几种疫苗合为一针，比如著名的麻风腮三联疫苗（MMR），即单板机疹、腮腺炎和风疹混合疫苗。他还研制出乙肝疫苗，而乙肝是肝癌主要成因之一，这是第一种抗癌疫苗。

最近费城儿童医院以希勒曼的名字设立了一个捐赠职位，在此之际他回顾了自己的工作。

“回首一生，你会说，‘嗨，我都干什么啦？我为世界所作的贡献是否足以证明我曾经活在这个世界上？’这是一大烦恼——至少对蒙大拿人来说，是这样。”

他接着说：“我要说，我对所有这一切感到很满意。我不是自鸣得意，不过我感到满意……我一周工作七天。如果再重来一次的话，我还愿意这样做，因为做一个有用的人其乐无穷，从中可以获得满足感。除此之外，这也是对科学和战胜这些病菌的追求。”

Hawking: One of the World's Leading Theoretical Physicists

Stephen William Hawking was born on 8 January 1942 (300 years after the death of Galileo) in Oxford, England. At eleven Stephen went to St. Albans School, and then on to University of Oxford, his father's old college. Stephen wanted to do Mathematics, although his father would have preferred medicine. Mathematics was not available at University College, so he did Physics instead. After three years and not very much work he was awarded a first class honors degree in Natural Science. Stephen then went on to Cambridge to do research in Cosmology, there being no one working in that area in Oxford at the time.

Stephen Hawking has worked on the basic laws which govern the universe. With Roger Penrose he showed that Einstein's General Theory of Relativity implied space and time would have a beginning in the Big Bang and an end in black holes. Thee results indicated it was necessary to unify General Relativity with Quantum Theory, the other great scientific development of the first half of the 20th Century. One consequence of such a unification he discovered was that black holes should not be completely black, but should emit radiation and eventually evaporate and disappear. Another conjecture is that the universe has no edge or boundary in imaginary time. This would imply that the way the universe began was completely determined by the laws of science.

Stephen Hawking is a rare celebrity scientist. He's even had a TV cameo role in *Star Trek* in which he plays poker with scientific icons Sir Isaac Newton and Albert Einstein. Yet when asked about comparisons between himself and the two scientists, he calls it all "media hype". Once he was asked how he felt about being labeled the world's smartest person, he responded: "It is very embarrassing. It is rubbish, just media hype. They just want a hero, and I fill the role model of a disabled genius. At least I am disabled, but I am no genius."

Hawking has ALS (amyotrophic lateral sclerosis), a neuromuscular disease that progressively weakens muscle control. As a 21-year-old graduate student in cosmology at

Cambridge University, doctors predicted an early death for him.

Today, he's 64 and married, with three children. He gets around in a wheelchair, and after completely losing the use of his vocal chords in an operation to assist his breathing in 1985, he communicates through a computer. A speech synthesizer "speaks" for him after he punches in what he wants to say, selecting words in the computer software by pressing a switch with his hand. Unfortunately, it makes him sound like he has an American accent, he says.

Despite his humorous, self-effacing manner, Hawking is one of the world's leading theoretical physicists. Many consider him to be the most brilliant since Einstein.

霍金：世界一流的理论物理学家

1942年1月8日，也就是伽利略逝世300周年的纪念日，斯蒂芬·威廉·霍金出生于英国牛津。11岁时，霍金进入圣·奥尔本斯中学学习，接着又升入父亲的母校牛津大学深造。父亲希望他攻读医科，年轻的斯蒂芬却想研究数学。但牛津的大学学院当时并未开设数学系，于是他转而研究起了物理。三年期满,他没怎么费力就拿到了一等自然科学荣誉学位。接着,他又去剑桥做起了宇宙学方面的研究,在当时的牛津,这还是个无人问津的学科。

斯蒂芬·霍金研究的是支配宇宙的基本法则。他和罗杰·彭罗斯一道证明:根据爱因斯坦的广义相对论,时间和空间必然始于大爆炸、终于黑洞。研究结果显示,必须将广义相对论同20世纪上半叶的另一项重大科学进展,即量子理论统一起来。霍金发现,两者一旦统一就会得出这样的结论:黑洞并非全黑,而是向外放出辐射,并将最终蒸发并消失。此外他还推测:宇宙在虚时间中无界限可言,根据这一点可知,宇宙创生的方式完全是由科学定律所决定的。

斯蒂芬·霍金是为数不多的科学名人之一。他甚至在《星际迷航记》中以本人的身份出镜,并在剧中同艾撒克·牛顿爵士和爱因斯坦这两位科学代言人玩了几局扑克。然而,当被问及自己和这两位科学家之间的异同时,霍金却将这个类比称为"媒体炒作"。有人曾问他对被奉为世上最聪明的人有何感受,他这样答道:"我觉得很难堪。这些都是胡说,是媒体的炒作。他们不过想要个英雄,我又像是个典型的残疾天才。残疾倒是没错,但我绝对不是天才。"

霍金患有ALS(全称"肌萎缩侧索硬化症"),这是一种神经肌肉方面的疾病,能逐步削弱肌肉的控制力。当21岁的他还在剑桥大学攻读宇宙学的研究生时,医生们就预言他必将早夭。

如今的他已经六十有四，结了婚，有了三个孩子，靠一张轮椅出入。1985 年，他接受了一次旨在辅助呼吸的手术，却在手术中完全失去了声带的功用，从此以一部电脑同外界交流：先用手按下开关，然后在计算机软件中选出合适的单词，组成想说的话，接着就由一台语音合成器代为发声。他说，不巧的是，这让他的语音染上了美国腔调。

霍金表面上幽默自谦，实际上却是世界一流的理论物理学家之一。在许多人眼里，他是继爱因斯坦之后最聪慧的人。

（高天羽　译）

II 作家和艺术家

Writers and Artists

Charles Dickens

When Charles Dickens was a small boy, he was sent by his parents to work in a boot-blacking factory. His parents had other children and many debts to pay.

Charles' father was put into prison for his debts. The boy tried to raise money enough to get him out but was unsuccessful. At last, the whole family went to live with Charles' father in his room in the Marshalsea Prison. This was a common practice and, while the prisoner could not leave the grounds, the families could go in and out freely until the gate was locked at night.

For the rest of his days, Dickens was interested in prisons. Whenever he traveled through strange towns and cities, he went to visit them, as other tourists would visit museums and palaces. Almost every book he wrote has a prison and some prisoners in it.

He had been born in 1812 and had stayed busy at one kind

of work or another from the time he was six years of age. He died of a sudden stroke in 1870. He provided the world with its clearest picture of the texture of English life during the 1800's, one without which readers would never know the sounds, smells, and tastes of those long-ago days.

Today Charles Dickens is considered one of the greatest English writers of all times. He is best remembered for his *Christmas Carol, David Copperfield,* and *Tale of Two cities.*

查尔斯·狄更斯

当查尔斯·狄更斯还是小孩的时候,他的父母就把他送到一家鞋油作坊去做工。他的父母还有其他孩子,负债累累。

查尔斯的父亲因债务被送进牢房。这个孩子尽力设法想挣到足够的钱使他父亲出狱,但是没有成功。最后,合家都搬到马歇尔西监狱他父亲的牢房里一起生活。这在当时是常有的事。犯人不能离开监狱营地,但家属在晚上锁门前可以自由出入。

此后,狄更斯对监狱仍很感兴趣。每当他旅行到陌生城镇的时候,他总要去访问监狱,就好像其他旅游者访问博物馆和宫殿一样。他写的每本书里,几乎都有监狱和囚犯。

他生于1812年。从6岁起,就忙着干这样那样的工作。1870年突然中风逝世。他向全世界提供了19世纪英国生活结构的最清晰的描绘。要是没有这种描绘,读者就无法了解那消逝已久的时代的声音、风味和人情。

今天,查尔斯·狄更斯被公认为英国历代最伟大的作家之一。他的作品《圣诞颂歌》、《大卫·科波菲尔》和《双城记》是最令人难忘的。

Ernest Hemingway

Ernest Hemingway was born on July 21, 1899, in the middle class suburb of Chicago, Illinois, called Oak Park. His father was a doctor of medicine, devoted to hunting and fishing; his mother was a religious woman, talented in music and painting. The doctor seems to have had the greater influence on the child. The parts of his boyhood that meant most to him were spent on summer vacations in Michigan, and are reflected in *the Nick Adams stories* — as, for the most part, his life-long rebellion against the intense Victorianism of Oak Park and both parents is not.

As a boy he learnt to box and he played high school football. He was not much pleased with the latter activity, however, partly because he was already more interested in writing. Working for his English classes and the school paper, he composed light verse, wrote a good many columns in imitation of Ring Lardner (a practice at which he became very adept), and tried his hand at some short stories. Although it looked for many years as though he was cut out to be a humorist, he also turned his hand to more serious fiction, and this is really the most impressive part of his juvenilia, already he was choosing to write about northern Michigan, and many of the feature of his later style — especially some of the earmarks of his famous dialogue — are discernible in this early prose.

Less exuberant and better-qualified testimony records the fact that he had genuine expertise in military matters, especially with regard to guerrilla activities and the collection of intelligence, and that he was extremely brave under fire.

But on other counts Hemingway as a man appears to have been complicated to the point of contradictions that have not yet been resolved. He was by turns witty, cheerful, and irascible, generous and selfish, expansive and self-centered as a tornado. This was a hedonist who worked, a stoic who suffered, a lover of life obsessed with death, a lifelong student and sportsman, a powerful, damaged man who basked and perspired in the limelight he alternately sought and shunned.

He was a gifted, strong personality, and at times *eccentric*. In *Across the River and into the Trees* Cantwell's eccentricities are the result of his having been so often injured. Although this diagnosis may seem both offhand and indirect, one of the consequences of Hemingway's physical adventures was that he was like Cantwell, physically long retained the record of about as many blows as a man may take and live. Understandably he did not wish to go down in history for this fact. But there seems little or no danger of that, and a list of his major injuries is certainly impressive and possibly significant. His skull was fractured at least once; he sustained at least a dozen brain concussions, several of them serious ones; he was in three bad automobile accidents; and several years prior to his death he was in two airplane accidents in the space of two days in the African jungle, during which time he suffered severe internal injuries, "jammed" his spine, and received a concussion so violent that his eyesight was impaired for some time. (It was on this occasion that quite a few newspapers printed obituaries, which he read, after his recovery, with great pleasure; the notices were favorable.) In warfare alone he was shot through nine parts of the body, and sustained six head wounds. When he was blown up in Italy at the age of eighteen, and was left, for a time, for dead, the doctors removed all of the 227 steel fragments which had penetrated him that they could get at.

Some amount of such gossip is relevant to any discussion of Hemingway's work if only because it confirms and informs the picture of him which the work has given us. Our view of that work is in turn informed and confirmed by modern psychology, which offers an account of how many of the things to be found in Hemingway come to be there. This is no place to go into the niceties and vagaries of contemporary psychoanalytic theory, much of it post-Freudian, but it is perhaps not out of place to remark that such theory does give an explanation of the preoccupations with Hemingway's books and life reflect. His hero's nightmares and insomnia (attendant on his first serious wounding), his preoccupation with death, and with the scene of what was nearly his own premature end, his devotion to hunting and fishing, his intellectual limitation — all these things and several others may be accounted for in psychoanalytic terms.

欧内斯特·海明威

1899 年 7 月 21 日，欧内斯特·海明威生于伊力诺伊州的芝加哥郊外橡树园的一个中产阶级家庭里。他的父亲是一位医学博士，酷爱打猎和钓鱼；他的母亲是位虔诚的基督教徒，极具音乐及绘画天赋。父母之中，父亲似乎对这个孩子的影响更大。他所珍爱的童年时光的一部分是在密歇根州的暑假生活中度过的，这些生活在他的《尼克·亚当斯的故事》中能找到影子，但他终生对橡树园的浓厚的清教气氛和对父母的反叛却没有在故事中得以体现。

他在孩提时代就开始学习拳击，高中时参加了校足球队。然而也许是因为更热衷于写作，海明威对足球提不起兴趣。在为英语课和校刊写作的时候，他常撰写小品文，并模仿拉德纳（海明威已非常驾轻就熟）的风格写了大量的专栏，同时还尝试着写了些短篇故事。尽管好多年来他好像被公认为幽默作家，但他也涉足一些严肃的文体，在他少年时期作品中，这些给人留下的印象最深刻。那时，他已经选择写些关于北密歇根的文章，而且很多后期作品的风格特点——尤其是他的有名的对话片段中的特点——在早期的散文作品中已表现得较为明显了。

辞藻不很华丽但字句铿锵的退伍证明记载了海明威在军旅生活中所表现出的非凡的特质，尤其涉及游击活动和搜集情报这些方面。同时，退伍证明还记载了他在战火下表现出的异常的英勇和威猛。

但如果考虑到其他方面的话，海明威这个人表现出的是一个永远调和不了的矛盾的统一体。风趣、快活、暴躁、慷慨、自私、率直和像龙卷风一样以自我为中心这些性格特征在他身上交替凸显。他是一个工作时的享乐主义者，一个遭受痛苦时的禁欲主义者，被死亡压抑的热爱生命的生灵，终生的学生和运动员，一个沐浴在他自己时而追寻又时而逃避的公众焦点的光环中坚强但屡遭打击的人。

他是一个天才，性格坚强，有时也很古怪。《过河入林》中的人物坎特威尔的古怪就是海明威经常受伤的结果。尽管这个判断显得唐突和缺乏实证，但海明威对于物质世界的探险经历的结果之一是，他像坎特威尔一样，保持着人无论在身体上遭受多少次打击仍可以存活的纪录。可以理解的是他并不希望因此而流芳百世。但好像几乎没有那种危险，他所经受的一长串的较大的伤残事故是骇人听闻的，同时可能是意义非常重大的。他的头骨曾经遭到至少一次粉碎性骨折；他遭受了至少12次的脑震荡，其中有几次是非常严重的；他遇到过3次恶性交通事故；就在海明威临死的前几年，他在非洲丛林里在两天之内遭遇了两次飞机事故，因此他受了严重的内伤，脊骨挫伤，重度脑震荡并发一段时间的视力损伤（在这种情况下，很多报纸刊出了他的讣告，康复之后，他非常欣喜地饶有兴致地读起来；这些讣闻是善意的）。仅在战争中他就被子弹射穿身体九个部分，造成六处脑伤。18岁时在意大利被炸伤的时候，海明威九死一生，医生们把能取出的弹片都从他身上取出来了,结果一共取出了227块。

每当讨论起海明威的作品时,一些闲言碎语就显得不可避免,只是因为这些事实能使我们通过他的作品了解到的海明威的形象更加清晰而有力。我们的观点是他的作品反过来被现代心理学的理论所印证,这些理论解释了为什么这么多事件都集中发生在海明威身上的原因。我们虽不应该误入大多后弗洛伊德的纷繁复杂的怪异的现代精神分析学的理论中,但是说这些理论确实可以解释海明威的作品和生活中反映出来的过分沉迷的心理现象是不过分的。他的主人公的梦魇和失眠(伴随着他的首次严重的伤害),他对死亡以及对自己过早的夭折的情景的过分关注,他对打猎和捕鱼的酷爱,他的智力的极限 —— 所有的这些还有其他我们没有提到的事实都可以正好用精神分析学的术语来解释。

Helen Keller: The Messenger of Courage and Hope

The name Helen Keller has special meaning for millions of people in all parts of the world. She could not see or hear. Yet she was able to do so much with life. Her success gave others hope.

Helen Keller was born on June 27, 1880, in a small town in Alabama. Her father, Arthur Keller, was a captain in the army of the south during the American Civil War. Her mother was his second wife.

Helen Keller was just like any other child until she was a year-and-a-half. She was very active. She began walking and talking early. Then, 19 months after she was born, Helen became very sick. It was a strange sickness that made her completely blind and deaf. The doctor could not do anything for her. Her bright, happy world now was filled with silence and darkness.

The young child had strong desires. She knew what she wanted to do. No one could stop her from doing it.

More and more, she wanted to communicate with others. Making simple signs with her hands was not enough. Something was ready to explode inside of her because she could not make people understand her. She screamed and struggled when her mother tried to control her.

When Helen was six, her father learned about a doctor in Baltimore, Maryland. The doctor had successfully treated people who were blind. Helen's parents took her on the train to Baltimore. The doctor said he could do nothing to help Helen. But he suggested the Kellers get a teacher for the blind who could teach Helen to communicate.

A teacher arrived from the Perkins Institution for the Blind in Boston. Her name was Anne Sullivan. She herself had once been almost completely blind, but had regained her sight. At Perkins, Miss Sullivan had learned the newest methods of teaching the blind.

Anne Sullivan began by teaching Helen that everything had a name. The secret to the names was the letters that formed them. The job was long and difficult. Helen had to learn how to use her hands and fingers to speak for her. First, she had to be taught how to obey and how to control her anger.

Miss Sullivan taught Helen many things, to read and write, and even to use a typewriter. The most important thing she taught Helen was how to think.

Helen learned more and more new words. All day, Miss Sullivan kept touching Helen's hand, spelling words that gave Helen a language. In time, Helen showed she could learn foreign languages. She learned Latin, Greek, French, and German.

Helen was able to learn many things, not just languages. She was never willing to leave a problem unfinished, even difficult problems in mathematics. One time, Miss Sullivan suggested leaving a problem to solve until the next day. But Helen wanted to keep trying. She said, "I think it will make my mind stronger to do it now."

Helen did go to college. She was 16 years old when she began studying at Radcliffe College in Cambridge, Massachusetts. She completed her studies with high honors. It was a hard struggle. Few of the books she needed were written in the Braille language that the blind read by touching pages. Miss Sullivan and others had to teach her what was in these books by forming words in her hands.

The study of geometry and physics was especially difficult. Helen could only learn about squares, triangles, and other geometrical shapes by making them with wires. She kept feeling the different shapes of the wires until she could see them in her mind.

During her second year at college, Miss Keller wrote the story of her life and what college meant to her. This is what she wrote: "My first day at Radcliffe College was of great interest. Some powerful force inside me made me test my mind. I wanted to learn if it was as good as that of others. I learned many things at college. One thing I slowly learned was that knowledge does not just mean power, as some people say. Knowledge leads to happiness, because to have it is to know what is true and real. To know what great men of the past have thought, said and done is to feel the heartbeat of humanity down through the ages."

All of Helen Keller's knowledge reached her mind through her sense of touch and smell and her feelings. Miss Keller learned to love things she could not hear — music for example. She did this through her sense of touch.

When waves of air beat against her, she felt them. Sometimes she put her hand to a singer's throat. She often stood for hours with her hands on a piano while it was played.

She also liked to go to museums. She thought she understood sculpture as well as others. Her fingers told her the true size and the feel of the material.

Helen Keller was tall and strong. When she spoke, her face looked very alive. She often felt the faces of close friends when she was talking to them, to discover their feelings. She and Miss Sullivan enjoyed jokes, laughing at funny things that happened to themselves or others.

Miss Keller had to work hard to support herself after she finished college in 1904. She worked for several organizations that helped blind people in America and in other countries. She started the Helen Keller Endowment Fund and asked for money from wealthy people. She wrote several books, and made a movie based on her life.

Miss Keller also worked to improve conditions for the blind in developing countries. After World War Ⅱ, she worked with soldiers who had been blinded in the fighting. She spoke in more than 25 countries. Her main goal was to increase public interest in the difficulties of people with physical problems.

Helen Keller died in 1968. She was 87 years old.

Organizations throughout the world continue her work. One of them is Helen Keller International. It has programs in more than 80 countries to prevent blindness, restore sight and improve life for the blind. It helps keep alive Helen Keller's message of courage and hope.

海伦·凯勒：勇气和希望的使者

海伦·凯勒这个名字对世界各地数百万的人来说都有着特殊的含义。她看不见也听不见，然而她一生中却能够做很多的事情。她的成功给其他人带来了希望。

海伦·凯勒于1880年6月27日出生在亚拉巴马州的一个小城镇。她的父亲，阿瑟·凯勒，是美国内战时期南方军队的一个上尉。海伦的母亲是他的第二任妻子。

在海伦一岁半以前，她与其他的小孩并没什么两样，她十分活跃，很早就学会走路和说话。但是在她19个月大的时候，海伦生了一场大病，奇怪的病使她完全丧失了视觉与听觉。医生对此无能为力。她原本光明、快乐的世界从此充满了沉寂与黑暗。

这个年轻的女孩有着一股强烈的欲望，她知道自己想要做什么，而且没有谁能够阻止她想要做的事。

海伦越来越想与别人交流，仅仅是做简单的手势已经不够。她内心有一些东西正准备爆发，因为她无法让人们理解她。当她母亲试着管束她时，她尖叫、挣扎。

当海伦6岁时，她父亲得知在马里兰州的巴尔的摩有位医生，他已成功地治愈了许多盲人。海伦的父母便把海伦带上了前往巴尔的摩的火车。可这位医生却说他对此也爱莫能助。医生建议凯勒夫妇为海伦找一个能够教会她如何交流的老师。

一位来自波士顿的帕金斯盲人研究所的老师来到了海伦家。她叫安妮·沙利文。她自己曾经几乎全盲，但后来又恢复了视力，在帕金斯研究所，沙利文小姐已经学会了教盲人的最新方法。

安妮·沙利文教导海伦是从告诉她每个事物都有它自己的名称开始的。而知道这些名称的诀窍就是要了解组成这些名称的字母，这是一项既艰难又漫长的工作。海伦不得不学会如何用她的手和手指说话。但刚开始，她不得不学会怎样服从，怎样去控制她的愤怒。

沙利文小姐教会了海伦很多事情——读、写、甚至使用打字机，最重要的是她教会了海伦如何思考。

海伦学会了越来越多的新单词。沙利文小姐整天都一直手把手地教海伦拼写单词，以此给她一种语言。经过一段时间以后，海伦显示出了她能够学习外国语。她学会了拉丁文、希腊文、法语与德语。

海伦能够学会很多东西，不仅仅是语言。她从不愿意半途而废，甚至对数学上的难题也是如此。一次，沙利文小姐建议海伦将一道难题留到第二天解决，但海伦却想继续尝试，她说："我认为现在将难题解决会使我的头脑更加灵活。"

海伦终于上了大学，当她在马萨诸塞州的剑桥瑞德克力夫大学学习时只有16岁。她以优等成绩修完了全部的课程。这是一场艰苦的抗争，她所需要的书没有几本是用那种靠触摸的供盲人阅读的盲文写的。沙利文小姐和其他的人不得不靠在她手心上拼划来告诉她书的内容。

几何和物理的学习是特别困难的。海伦只能靠用钢丝围出图形的方式去了解正方形、三角形和其他一些几何图形。她总是不停地去感受、去揣摩钢丝所围成的不同图形，直到她能在自己头脑中将它们勾画出来。

在大学的第二年里，凯勒小姐写下了她生活的故事以及大学对她的影响。这是她所写的："在瑞德克力夫大学的第一天，我的内心充满了无比的新奇。我内心有一股强大的力量促使我去审视自己，我想知道我的头脑是不是和别人的一样。在大学里，我学到了不少知识。我慢慢地懂得了一件事情，知识并不仅仅像人们所说的那样意味着力量，知识还会使人幸福，因为拥有知识就能知道什么是真的和实在的。了解过去那些伟人们想过些什么、说过些什么、做过些什么，就能感受到在过去那些岁月中人类的心跳。”

海伦·凯勒所有的知识都是通过她的触觉、她的嗅觉和她的内心感受传送到大脑的，凯勒小姐学会了去热爱她听不见的事物，譬如音乐，而且她是通过她的触觉来学会的。

当空气振动时，她能从声波感受到音乐的流动。有时，她把手放在演唱者的喉咙上。当别人弹奏钢琴时，她经常把手放在钢琴上，在旁边站很久。

她还喜欢去博物馆。她认为她能够像其他人那样很好地理解雕塑，欣赏雕塑。她的手指告诉她真实的尺寸与材料的触感。

海伦·凯勒个子很高，身体也很强壮。当她说话时，她的脸看上去十分生动。当她与亲密朋友交谈时，就会用手去触摸他们的脸来感受他们的情感。她与沙利文小姐很喜欢开玩笑，时常会对发生在她俩身上的或是其他人身上的趣事而开怀大笑。

凯勒小姐在1904年完成她的大学学业后，不得不努力工作来维持生计。她为美国和其他国家的几个帮助盲人的组织工作。她创设了海伦·凯勒资助基金，并从富人们那里获得募捐，她写了几本书，并根据她自己的生活经历拍了一部电影。

凯勒小姐也致力于改善发展中国家盲人生活条件的工作。二战过后，她做战争中失明的士兵们的工作。她在25

个以上的国家和地区都发表过演讲。她的主要目标是要提高公众对残疾人生活困难的关注。

海伦·凯勒于1968年离开了人世,享年87岁。

全世界的许多组织都在继续着她的未竟事业。其中有一个就是"海伦·凯勒国际",它在80多个国家都设有分支机构来防止变盲,帮助盲人重获光明并改善他们的生活。它使海伦·凯勒的勇气与信念长存人间。

Da Vinci: One of the Greatest Painters

Over five hundred years ago, a man designed a flying machine. He also invented a helicopter. This clever man was an Italian. He was called Leonardo Da Vinci.

In 1480, Da Vinci wrote to the ruler of Milan asking for work. He said he was a good painter and sculptor. He also designed bridges. He made weapons, too. He even invented machine guns. Eventually he got a job in Milan as a musician.

He was good at everything he tried. We remember him today, however, as an artist. He was one of the greatest artists the world have ever produced. You may have heard of a picture called *Mona Lisa.* He painted that. While he was in Milan, he painted a special picture. He drew it on the wall of a monastery dining room. Many people say this picture is the greatest one ever painted. It's called *The Last Supper.* Da Vinci worked hard painting this picture. Often he worked all day and never stopped to eat or drink.

He walked about the city of Milan with a notebook in his hand. He drew pictures of people in the street who interested him. He also watched the way birds and insects fly. He wanted to know how everything worked. He even made plans for rebuilding Milan. Like modem architects, he wanted towns to be light and airy. He planned the main roads on two levels. One road was for pedestrians, the other for traffic.

We have very little of his work today. Da Vinci finished only a few of his paintings. He left many unfinished because he thought they were not perfect. No one in his lifetime knew how great Da Vinci was. We now believe, however, that he was one of the cleverest men the world have ever known.

达·芬奇：最伟大的画家

500 多年前有一个人设计了一台飞行器，他还发明了直升机。这个聪明人就是意大利人，他的名字叫列奥纳多·达·芬奇。

1480 年，达·芬奇给米兰的统治者写了一封信，要求给他一份工作。他说自己是一个优秀的画家和雕刻家，还能设计桥梁,也能制造武器,甚至发明了机关枪。最后他在米兰得到一份乐师的工作。

他不管干什么工作都干得很出色。不过今天我们主要将他当作一位画家记在心里。他是世界上出现过的最伟大的画家之一。你可能听说过有一幅叫《蒙娜·丽莎》的名画。那就是他画的。他在米兰的时候,画了一幅特别的画。他是在一座修道院餐厅的墙上画这幅画的。许多人说这是世界上最伟大的一幅画,它叫作《最后的晚餐》。画这幅画时,达·芬奇工作非常勤奋。他常常一画就是一整天,连吃饭喝水都不肯停笔。

他常常带着一个笔记本在米兰街上走,看到让他感兴趣的人他就画。他还观察鸟类和昆虫怎样飞翔。他想知道一切事物活动的原理。他甚至还制定了改建米兰的计划。他和现代的建筑师一样,希望城市鲜亮空气好。他把主要街道都设计成两层:一层人行道,另一层车道。

我们今天保存他的作品很少。在达·芬奇的画中,他只完成了几幅。许多画他都没有画完,因为他认为它们不够完美。在他活着的时候,没有人知道达·芬奇有多么伟大,但是现在我们都认为他是世界上出现过的最聪明的人之一。

Van Gogh: An Impressionist

Vincent Van Gogh was a man in a hurry, an artist of tremendous energy and prodigious output. He killed himself when he was only 37, but he left behind him more than 2,000 paintings and drawings, which established his reputation in a way he would never have considered possible.

Van Gogh was born on March 30, 1853 at Groot Zundert in the Dutch Province of Noord Brabant. He was the son of a clergyman. His first artistic impressions were formed as a boy, from his uncle who was an art dealer. The motivations bore early fruit and from the age of 12 the young Vincent was drawing. The interest led to an apprenticeship in an art dealer's firm, Groupil's, in the Hague. When he was only 20, he was transferred to the firm's London office.

In London Van Gogh faced his first major crisis, when he was rejected in love. After that, he turned to religion, expressed disapproval with art-dealing and neglected his work.

Groupil transferred him from London to Paris, but when his work was still unsatisfactory, dismissed him in 1876.

The young Van Gogh made religion a consuming interest and during the next few years traveled in Britain, Belgium and Holland, trying to establish himself as a preacher, but without success. He developed strong opinions on social morality, customs and church life and alienated those he mixed with by an uncompromising attitude.

In 1880, at the age of 27, he found himself drawn back to art. He had a job as an assistant evangelist in the mining village of Borinage in Belgium but realized an artistic drive which was to motivate him unceasingly until his death 10 years later.

Although he returned to Noord Brabant and his family early in 1881, his first recognized works were set in Borinage and reflected the rural culture in which he was living and his belief in order and symmetry in both society and art. The period resulted in what became known as the Brabant canvases.

At this time he was becoming obsessed with artistic development. Although he was limited in practical experience, his work showed confidence and maturity from the start, no doubt influenced by the strength of his personal convictions within the family, now that he was living back with his parents in Brabant. He was short of money and rebelling against social and academic standards.

Late in 1881 he moved to the Hague and established a relationship with a woman, Christine Hoornik, with whom he lived for a time. He broke with her in 1883, however, and never again established a significant intimate relationship with a woman.

Between 1883 and 1886, at Noord Brahant again, his painting developed into characteristic dark landscapes and scenes of country life. He stressed character and expression rather than perspective and physical accuracy, he was already experimenting with impressionism.

In 1886 Van Gogh left Holland forever and traveled via Antwerp to Paris, and to major changes in artistic style. Van Gogh's work became more youthful in Paris. He lived with his brother, Theo, who managed the modern department of an art dealer's. A new, more animated, painting style emerged and the impressionist tendencies of earlier work weakened somewhat.

Van Gogh developed a taste for personalized brushwork and brilliant, unmixed colours. Among his most *prominent* experiments with colour were a series of some 30 flower paintings, a *fascination* which stayed with him until his death.

凡·高：印象派画家

温森特·凡·高，这位精力充沛、激情澎湃的高产画家，匆忙地度完了自己的艺术人生。年仅37岁时，他自杀身亡，身后留下了2 000多幅绘画作品，这些作品使他名满天下，其程度是凡·高生前无论如何也没有料想到的。

1853年3月30日，凡·高生于荷兰诺得·布拉邦特省的一个名叫格鲁特·松丹特的小村子里。他的父亲是位牧师。凡·高对绘画产生的最初印象是受他做画商的叔父的熏陶，当时他还是个孩子。在这种熏陶下，凡·高做画的动机早早地就形成了，12岁时，年轻的温森特已经开始习画了。对绘画的兴趣使他在海牙的一个名叫古比尔的画店当了学徒。年仅20岁的时候，他又被调往这家公司的伦敦总部。

在伦敦，凡·高经历了生命中的第一次挫折，他被爱情拒绝了。此后，他开始转向忙于宗教，而对于以追求利益最大化的商业美术表现出了不屑的态度，对工作玩忽职守。古比尔公司因此把他从伦敦调到巴黎，但在那里，他的工作仍然不能令人满意，于是在1876年，凡·高被解雇了。

年轻的凡·高对宗教产生了强烈的兴趣，在接下来的几年里，他游历了英国、比利时以及荷兰，他试着使自己成为一名教士，但他失败了。他所持有的有关社会道德、风俗及宗教生活的偏执的观点，与周围的人格格不入。

1880年，在他27岁时，凡·高发现有种力量吸引着自己重操画业。他得到了一份去比利时的波里纳日矿区当义务传教士的工作，在那儿，他意识到自己被一种艺术创作的冲动所驱使着，这种冲动在他死前的10年里无时无刻不在激励着他，一刻都没有停止过。

虽然凡·高于1881年年初就回到了诺得·布拉邦特，回到了家人的身边，但他最初得到认可的作品仍然是在波里纳日创作的，这些作品反映了他曾经生活过的乡村文化、他虔诚的信仰以及社会与艺术的调和。后来，这一阶段被称为布拉邦特油画时代。

这一时期，他对绘画艺术的发展到了心醉神迷的程度。虽然他只局限于绘画的实践，但他的作品从一开始就表现出了自信和成熟，这无疑是受他在家中的坚定的个性所影响。现在他又回到布拉邦特，与父母亲住在一起。他经济拮据，与社会及当时认可的绘画艺术标准背道而驰。

1881年年末，他移居海牙，在那与一个名叫克里丝汀·霍尼克的女人建立了关系，同居了一段时间后，1883年，他们分手了。此后，凡·高再没有与任何女人有过亲密的关系。

1883 年到 1886 年,凡·高重返布拉邦特,他的绘画发展成了个性鲜明但线条模糊的风景画,有的也表现乡村生活。他重点强调的是人物和表情而不是透视法和实体的准确度,他已经在实践印象主义了。

1886 年,凡·高永远地离开了荷兰,取道安特卫普到巴黎,同时他的绘画风格经历了巨大的改变。凡·高的作品在巴黎开始变得新鲜活泼了。他和弟弟提奥住在一起,当时提奥正负责经营一个画店的现代画部门。一种全新的、更活泼的绘画风格应运而生了,印象派的早期作品中的倾向在一定程度上减弱了。

凡·高发展了一种个性化笔法和纯色鲜艳的审美品位。最能鲜明突出地表现其色彩风格的是他的一系列以花为题材的 30 幅绘画作品,这些作品是他迷恋的东西,一直陪伴着他,直到他走到艺术生命的尽头。

Picasso: The Youngest Artist

Pablo Picasso was a pioneer, a master and a protean master, with a hand in every art movement of the century. He was born in Malaga, Spain in 1881. When he died in 1973, he was ninety-one years old. But he still took up his paints and brushes to start a new picture as if he were seeing things for the first time.

That's why we have called him the youngest painter. Young people are always trying new things and new ways of doing things. They don't hesitate to attempt one thing after another. Eager to experiment, they welcome new ideas. They are restless and alive and never satisfied. They seek perfection.

When he was over ninety, this great painter still lived his life like a young man. He was still restlessly looking for new ideas and for new ways to use his artistic materials. No one knew what to expect from him next. No one could be sure what kind of picture he would produce. If he had painted a picture of you, it might have looked exactly like you. Or it might have been all lines, squares, circles and strange-colored shapes. It might not have looked like human at all.

At such times Picasso was trying to paint what he saw with his mind as well as with his eyes. He put in the side of the face as well as the front. He might have painted it flat, as though it had no depth. Sometimes he seemed to paint just as a child paints, simply for his own pleasure. He didn't imitate others. " If the subjects I have wanted to express have suggested different ways of expression, I have never hesitated to use them." he said.

Most painters discover a style of painting that suits them and stick to that, especially if people admire their pictures. As the artist grows older his pictures may change, but not very much. But Picasso was like a man who had not yet found his own particular style of painting. He was still struggling to find perfect expression for his own uneasy spirit.

If ever anyone was born to be a painter, Picasso was. His father was a painter and art teacher who gave his son his first lessons in drawing. Picasso won a prize for his first important painting, "Science and Charity", when he was only fifteen. He studied art in several cities in Spain. But there was no one to teach him all he wanted to know. When he was nineteen, he visited Paris.

Paris was then the centre of the world for artists. Everything that was new and exciting in the world of painting seemed to happen there. When he was twenty-three, Picasso returned there to live and lived in France for the rest of his life.

But life was not easy for an unknown painter. The struggle began to show in a new choice of subjects. For several years he painted people from the poorer parts of the city. He painted men and women who were thin, hungry, tired, sick and blind. His colours got darker. Most of these pictures were painted in shades of blue and showed very clearly what the artist saw and felt. The paintings of this "blue period" are full of pity and despair.

Picasso did not have to wait long for success. As he began to sell his pictures and to become recognized as a painter, his pictures took on a warmer look. At the same time he began to paint with more and more freedom and independence. He began to see people and places in simple forms and shapes. He no longer tried to make his pictures true-to-life.

The results at first seemed strange and unreal. The pictures were difficult to understand. He painted human heads, scenes from nature, or ordinary objects all in the same way: as if their shapes were the one important thing about them. This style of painting, which spread to many other artists, was known as Cubism.

Picasso painted thousands of pictures in many different styles. Sometimes he painted the natural look of things. Sometimes he seemed to break them apart. He demanded the right to show us what the mind knows as well as what the eye sees. He himself remained as curious about the world as he had been when he was young.

毕加索：最年轻的艺术家

巴伯罗·毕加索是一位先锋、一位名家，也是一位多才多艺的宗师，他的身影出现在 20 世纪的所有艺术运动中。他于 1881 年生在西班牙的马拉加，1973 年辞世，享年 91 岁。他在临终前还手持颜料画笔，准备创作一幅新的画作，仿佛正第一次看见这个世界。

这就是我们为什么把他称为“最年轻的艺术家”。年轻人总是在尝试新鲜事物，尝试做事的新方法。他们毫不犹豫地进行一次次的尝试。他们急于试验，总是欢迎新的想法。他们从不停歇，充满活力，永不满足。他们追求完美。

大画家年过九旬还生活得像一个年轻人，依然在不断寻找使用艺术素材的新想法和新手段。没人知道他下一步会创造出什么来，也没人能确定他还会画出什么样的作品。要是他给你画了幅肖像画，它可能和你一模一样，也可能充满了线段、方块、圆形和色彩怪异的物体，还可能与人类没有丝毫相像。

这个时期的毕加索不仅是在用双眼，也是在用心灵作画。他将脸的侧面和正面放进同一张画里。他会将人脸画成扁平，仿佛它没有深度。有时候，他的画作犹如儿童的涂鸦，完全是为了让自己开心。他从不模仿别人。他曾经说：“如果我要表达的主题还有其他的表达方式，我就会毫不犹豫地进行尝试。”

大多数画家会发掘一种适合自己的绘画风格，然后固守不变，当他们的画作受人喜爱时尤其如此。等到年事稍长，他们的画风可能有所转变，但不会变化太多。然而，毕加索却像是还没有找到自己独特的画风，他仿佛还在努力寻找一种风格，以充分表达他那不安分的灵魂。

如果有人生来就是画家，那就是毕加索。他的父亲是一位画家，也是位艺术教师，是他给自己的儿子上了第一堂绘画课。毕加索年仅 15 岁就画出了他的第一件重要作品《科学与慈悲》,并以此赢得了一尊奖杯。他在西班牙的几个城市学习过美术,但没人教得了他想知道的一切。19 岁那年,他去了巴黎。

当时的巴黎是全世界艺术家的中心。绘画界中一切内容新颖、振奋人心的事件似乎都在那里发生。23 岁时,毕加索回到巴黎居住,他的余生都在法国度过。

但对于一位籍籍无名的画家而言,生活并不容易。他开始选择新的主题来表现生活中的挣扎。他一连几年都为赤贫街区的市民画像。他画过形形色色的男男女女,瘦的、饿的、倦的、病的、盲的,下笔的色彩日益黯淡。这些画作大多以蓝色绘就,艺术家的所见所感呼之欲出。怜悯和绝望充斥在这个“蓝调时期”的作品当中。

没等多久,毕加索就迎来了成功。他的画作开始售出,也逐渐被人们视为画家,这个时期,他的作品变得温暖起来,画风也日趋自由独立。他开始着眼人和场所的简单外观和形状,不再试图让画作显得逼真了。

起初,这些画作显得离奇而不真实,叫人难以理解。在画面上,无论人头、自然景观,还是寻常物体都用单一的手法绘就:形状仿佛成了唯一重要的元素。这种画风在许多艺术家中流传开来,并获得了“立体主义”的称号。

毕加索画了数千幅作品,变换过许多种风格。他时而画出物体的天然外观，时而又将它们分解拆散。他向我们展示了双眼所见，也呈现了心灵所知。同年轻时相比，他对世界的好奇一直未曾改变。

（高天羽　译）

Ludwing Van Beethoven

Ludwing Van Beethoven was born in Bonn, Germany, on December 16, 1770. His father and grandfather were both musicians.

Beethoven revealed his own musical talents when he was very young. At the age of 7, he was playing in public.

In 1787, Beethoven traveled to Vienna and met his idol, Mozart. After playing a little on the harpsichord, he asked for a theme, on which he improvised so wonderfully that Mozart listened with interest and said, turning to the other musicians present: "This young man will leave his mark in the world some day."

But Beethoven could not stay in Vienna. His mother fell ill, and he rushed back to Bonn.

In 1792, Beethoven returned to Vienna, where he spent the rest of his life. He became Haydn's pupil, but was dissatisfied with his method of teaching. In order not to offend the famous master, he took lessons in secret from another compose, Joan Schenk.

Beethoven soon became famous. Then tragedy struck. He discovered that he was slowly becoming deaf. This was the great crisis of his life.

After this, Beethoven's music became more profound. He developed a completely original style of composing. It reflected his violent emotions, his sufferings, and joys. At this time Beethoven composed the most popular of all symphonies, his fifth, *Fate*, in which he expressed a musical depiction of his struggle with the fate of deafness. He dedicated his Symphony No. 3, *Heroic*, to Napoleon, thinking he stood for "Liberty, Equality and Fraternity", for he deeply sympathized with the ideals of the French Revolution. But the moment he heard that Napoleon had declared himself Emperor, he tore out the dedication on the title page.

It was during this last period of his life that he produced some of his greatest, most thoughtful works, among which was Symphony No. 9.

In 1826, Beethoven became seriously ill; and on March 26, 1827, he died, at the age of 57. He said, before his death, "In heaven I shall hear."

Twenty-five thousand people lined the streets through which was carried the bier of the greatest composer the world has ever known. There were thirty torchbearers, among them Franz Schubert, with other well-known musicians, artists, authors and poets.

In the old cemetery in Vienna can be seen the Master's last resting place, which contains a simple monument on which is engraved the glorious name: Beethoven.

The life of Beethoven is the life of a great artist who was also a great man. His genius enlarged the language of music, for his compositions speak to the world of the struggles, aspirations and triumphs of the soul. They are deeply emotional and express the feelings of all humanity in their beauty. His character was a noble one. People respect him for his great genius and love him for the goodness and purity of his soul. Through grief and misfortune he bravely fought a lifelong battle with fate in order to be worthy of his high ideals. He was a man of profound vision and his music has deeply moved its listeners for generations.

路德维希·凡·贝多芬

路德维希·凡·贝多芬1770年12月16日出生在德国波恩。他的父亲和爷爷都是音乐家。

贝多芬还很小的时候就显露出音乐才华。7岁时,贝多芬已登台表演了。

1787年,贝多芬到了维也纳,见到了他崇拜的偶像莫扎特。贝多芬在大键琴上演奏了一会儿后,又要了个主旋律。他即兴演奏得很出色,莫扎特听得兴致勃勃,转身对其他在场的音乐家说:"这个年轻人有一天会在世界上留下英名。"

但是,贝多芬不能待在维也纳,因为母亲病了,便匆匆赶回波恩。

1792年,贝多芬重返维也纳,在那里度过了他的余生。他成了海顿的学生,但不满意海顿的教学方法。为了不得罪这位大师,他暗中从师于另一位作曲家约翰·申克。

贝多芬很快成名了。后来,悲剧发生了,他发现自己在慢慢变聋。这是他生命中的巨大危机。

从此,贝多芬的音乐内涵更加深刻了。他创造了一种全新的作曲风格。他的音乐反映了他激荡的思想感情、痛苦和欢乐。在此期间,贝多芬创作了交响乐中最著名的第五交响曲《命运》。在这支交响曲中,他用音乐描述了他对失聪命运的抗争。贝多芬非常赞同法国大革命的理想,因此他把第三交响曲《英雄》献给拿破仑,认为拿破仑代表着“自由、平等和博爱”。但是,当他听说拿破仑宣布称帝时,立刻撕去了写着献词的扉页。

正是在贝多芬生命的最后时期,他创作了一些最伟大、最富有思想内涵的作品,其中包括第九交响曲。

1826 年,贝多芬病情严重了;1827 年 3 月 26 日贝多芬去世,享年 57 岁。临终前,他说:“在天堂,我会听见声音。”

这位世界上有史以来最伟大的作曲家的棺木从街道两旁站立的 2.5 万人中抬过。30 位著名的音乐家、艺术家、作家和诗人手持火炬,其中有弗朗兹·舒伯特。

在维也纳古老的公墓里,可以看到这位大师的最后安息地——一块简朴的石碑,石碑上刻着那个辉煌的名字:贝多芬。

贝多芬的一生是一位伟大艺术家的一生,也是一个伟人的一生。他的天赋丰富了音乐的语言;他的作品向全世界宣讲这个伟大灵魂的挣扎、抱负和胜利,深深地感动着人们,表达了整个人类的美的感情。他的人品高尚。人们尊敬他的伟大才华,热爱他心灵的善良和纯洁。为了不愧于自己崇高的理想，他在痛苦和不幸中跟命运英勇地进行了一生的抗争。他是一个有着深刻思想的人，他的音乐深深地感动了一代代的听众。

Johann Strauss

Johann Strauss was born in Vienna in 1825. His father, a well-known musician, was a strange and moody man. He did not want any of his children to be musicians. He whipped young Johann because the boy insisted he wanted to study music. At last, Johann left his family permanently. He grieved over leaving the family because the wonderful music he always had with him at home was gone forever. The only good thing about the family separation, it seemed, was that young Johann would be free to study music.

The dance called the waltz developed from a peasant dance in three-quarter time. The waltz became popular in Vienna, so it was only natural that Johann would be attracted to it.

The orchestra Johann's father had directed was prepared to disband when the elder Strauss suddenly died. Young Johann offered to take his father's place. Most of the musicians questioned that a young man would expect to fill the shoes of a famous father. They did not take into consideration that the son already had an orchestra of his own which was becoming well-known. Finally, one of the members persuaded the others to let the two orchestras be combined. Their first performance was a memorial concert played in his father's honor.

Soon Vienna was paying tributes to the son. He wrote such famous waltzes as *Tales from the Vienna Woods* and *The Beautiful Blue Danube,* and his music is still played today. His waltzes are as beautiful and timely as when Strauss first wrote them.

约翰·施特劳斯

约翰·施特劳斯 1825 年生于维也纳。他的父亲是著名音乐家，性情怪僻易怒。他不喜欢他的孩子成为音乐家。他鞭挞小约翰，因为这孩子坚持说他要学音乐。终于，小约翰永远地离开了家庭。他感到十分伤心，因为家中一直陪伴他的美妙的音乐从此一去不复返了。离开家园唯一的好处是小约翰可以自由自在地学习音乐了。

一种叫作华尔兹的舞蹈是从 3/4 拍的农家舞蹈发展而

来的。华尔兹在维也纳很流行，所以小约翰很自然地被吸引住了。

由于老施特劳斯突然亡故，他所指挥的管弦乐队准备解散。小约翰提出要接替他父亲的位置。大多数音乐家对这位年轻人要继承著名的父亲的衣钵抱有怀疑。他们没有想到他已经拥有自己的管弦乐队，而且是崭露头角的乐队。最后，有一个乐队成员说服了其他人员，把两个乐队合并起来。他们的首次演出是为他父亲举行的纪念音乐会。

不久这位儿子就誉满维也纳。他写下了著名的圆舞曲，像《维也纳森林的故事》、《美丽的蓝色多瑙河》等。施特劳斯的音乐今天仍然在演奏。他的圆舞曲美妙时行，不减当年。

Mythical Elvis Presley

When Elvis Presley died on August 16, 1977, he began to be recognized as an American myth. Today, there are over 625 active Elvis fan clubs worldwide. Graceland, Elvis's home and eternal resting place, is a shrine for many of his fans. Welcoming almost 700,000 visitors each year, the mansion is one of the most-visited historic homes in America.

So why, after all these years, is the world stuck on Elvis? The answer lies in culture: Elvis Presley is American myth personified. He is greater than the sum of his songs and movies; he symbolizes the American dream. Born in poverty, Elvis used his innate talent to rise above his condition and achieve his dream, without coming from a socially connected, politically powerful, or wealthy family. Globally, he has sold over ten billion records, more than any other artist, only to die young and leave behind a growing legion of fans.

Those fans choose to overlook Elvis drug dependency and

other excessive behaviour, preferring instead to recall what they see as his better nature. During his lifetime, Elvis donated money to charities and bought gifts for the poor and for his family and friends. Furthermore, the hometown boy, young Elvis, who made good, never left the comfort of Memphis, always keeping close to his roots, remembering the people and places from which he came.

神话般的猫王

猫王艾尔维斯·普雷斯利于1977年8月16日辞世。与此同时,他成为美国的神话。如今,全世界的猫王歌迷俱乐部达625家之多。Graceland是猫王的家,也是他永久的休息地。同时,对于猫王的歌迷来说,这里是他们的圣地。他的宅邸是美国接待游客最多的历史遗迹,这里每年要接待70万名拜访者。

那么,猫王为什么在离开我们这么久以后,还能保持如此的吸引力呢?这个问题的答案跟文化有关:普雷斯利是拟人化的美国神话。他本人要比他的歌曲和电影还伟大,他象征着美国梦。他不是出生在一个社会关系复杂、政治势力庞大或经济状况殷实的家庭。出身贫寒的他完全凭借个人的才华脱颖而出,实现了自己的梦想。他的唱片的发行量超过了100亿张,超过了其他任何一位艺术家。遗憾的是,他过早地离开了我们,只留下越来越多的追随者。

这些歌迷不愿意过分注重他吸毒的事实和其他的过激行为,他们宁愿看到他更好的一面。比如,他活着的时候曾经向慈善机构捐款,为穷人、他的家人和朋友买礼品。成名后的艾尔维斯从来没有忘记他的家乡孟斐斯,他的根一直在那里,他会永远地记住那个地方和那里的人民。

Chaplin: The Little Tramp

Charlie Chaplin was born on April 16, 1889 in London. His father was an entertainer and although not one of the big names, he was doing very well. His mother Hannah was also an entertainer. A wonderful mimic, she had a sweet, charming voice. While they were by no means rich, the music hall provided the Chaplins with a comfortable living.

Unfortunately happy life didn't last long. Father's alcoholism was slowly, but surely destroying his marriage. Finally it ended in divorce, but Hannah was indomitable. Without her, Charlie Chaplin would have become just one more child lost in the poverty of Victorian London. Somehow she not only managed to keep Charlie and his brother Syney clean and warm, clothed and fed but she conjured little treats for them. She would sit at the window watching the passersby and guess at their characters from the way they looked and behaved, spinning tales to delight Charlie and Syney. Charlie took in her skills and went on using them all his life.

Charlie had always believed, even in the worst times, that he had something special locked away inside him. He took his courage and went to see one of the top theatrical agents. With no experience at all, he was being offered the plum part of Billy — the pageboy in a new production of *Sherlock Holmes*. *Sherlock Holmes* opened on July 27, 1903 at the enormous Pavilion Theatre Charlie seemed to change overnight. It was as if he had found the thing he was meant to do.

It was, by now, 1908, Charlie was nineteen and he fell in love. Hetty Kelly was only fifteen. But her parents quashed the romance before it really begun — but the memory of pretty Hetty stayed with Charlie all his life.

In 1910, when Karno set off on his yearly American tour, "One of the best pantomime artists ever seen here." They had reached Philadelphia when a telegram arrived and he was being offered the chance to replace a star in the Keystone film company.

Cinema was born in the same year as Charlie thought people still believed it was a passing fad, and would never replace live shows. He was kept hanging about for several weeks and he used the time to watch and to learn. He was determined to master this new medium. It offered him the chance of money and success — and it would set him free from the unpredictability of live audience.

Charlie's first film, released in February 1914, was called *Making a living*. Though it didn't satisfy Charlie, the public liked it. After that he had made ten films and he had learned a lot. The public loved him and distributors were demanding more and more Chaplin films. In an incredibly short time, Charlie had become a very important man in motion picture . . .

卓别林：小小流浪汉

查理·卓别林于1889年4月16日出生在伦敦。他的父亲是位艺人，没有名列一线，但表现不俗。母亲汉娜同样是艺人，她是位出色的滑稽演员，声音甜美迷人。卓别林一家虽然不算富裕，但剧院的酬劳还是让他们的日子过得舒舒服服。

不幸的是，幸福的生活并没有持续多久。父亲贪恋酒精，这个嗜好缓慢地毁掉了他的婚姻。父母两人最终以离异收场，但汉娜并未就此消沉。要不是她，查理·卓别林就会成为维多利亚时期的又一名贫儿。她不仅设法让查理和他兄弟西德尼吃饱穿暖、打扮得干干净净，还为他们带来了欢乐。她常常坐在窗前注视来往的路人，并从他们的外表和举止猜出他们的性格，还会编故事逗乐查理和西德尼。查理学会了她的技艺，受用终身。

查理始终相信自己体内藏着特殊的潜能，即便在最糟的时候也是如此。他鼓起勇气去拜见了一位顶尖戏剧经纪人。完全没有演出经验的他得到了一份意外的美差——在新版《福尔摩斯》中扮演听差比利。《福尔摩斯》于 1903 年 7 月 27 日在盛大的帕威廉剧院开演。查理仿佛在一夜之间变了个人。他似乎找到了自己注定要做的事。

时间到了 1908 年，19 岁的查理恋爱了。心上人海蒂·凯利只有 15 岁。女孩的父母将这段恋情扼杀在了萌芽之中，但海蒂的倩影终生萦绕在查理的记忆中。

1910 年，老板卡诺率剧团踏上了一年一度的美国巡演，此时的卓别林已经成了“美国一流的哑剧表演艺术家”。剧团到达费城时收到了一封电报，启斯东电影公司给了卓别林一个机会，让他取代本公司某位影星的位置。

电影诞生的那年，查理觉得它在人们眼中不过是一时的潮流，不可能取代现场表演的地位。他有几个礼拜没有工作，在这段时间里，他看电影、学电影，并决心掌握这种新媒体。电影不仅给他带来了财富和成功——还有，他再也不用面对变化无常的现场观众了。

查理的首部电影《谋生之路》于 1914 年 2 月发行。查理对它并不满意，但观众却很喜欢。在那以后，他又拍了十部电影，并从中学到了许多。公众爱他，发行商则不断索要他的新片。查理转眼就成了电影界的重要人物……

（高天羽　译）

Chanel: Fashion Designer

Chanel would not have defined herself as a feminist in fact, she consistently spoke of femininity rather than of feminism yet her work is unquestionably part of the liberation of women. She threw out a life jacket, as it were, to women not once but twice, during two distinct periods decades apart: the 1920s and the 1950s. She not only appropriated styles, fabrics and articles of clothing that were worn by men but also, beginning with how she dressed herself, appropriate sports clothes as part of the language of fashion. One can see how her style evolved out of necessity and defiance. She couldn't afford the fashionable clothes of the period — so she rejected them and made her own, using, say, the sports jackets and ties that were everyday male attire around the racetrack, where she was climbing her first social ladders.

Throughout the 1920s, Chanel's social, sexual and professional progress continued, and her eminence grew to the status of legend. By the early 1930s she'd been courted by Hollywood, gone and come back. She had almost married one of the richest men in Europe, the Duke of Westminster; when she didn't, her explanation was, "there have been several Duchesses of Westminster. There is only one Chanel." In fact, there were many Coco Chanels, just as her work had many phases and many styles, including Gypsy skirts, over-the-top fake jewelry and glittering evening wear made of crystal and jet beads laid over black and white georgette crepe — not just the plainer jersey suits and "little black dresses" that made her famous. But probably the single element that most ensured Chanel's being remembered even when it would have been easier to write her off, is not a piece of clothing but a form of liquid gold — Chanel No. 5, in its Art Deco bottle, which was launched in 1923. It was the first perfume to bear a designer's name.

By the late 1960s, Chanel had become part of what she once rebelled against and hated — the Establishment. But if one looks at documentary footage of her from that period. one can still feel the spit and vinegar of the fiery peasant woman who began her fashion revolution against society by aiming at the head, with hats. Her boyish "flapper" creations were in sharp contrast to the Belle Epoque millinery that was in vogue at the time, about which she asked, "How can a brain function under those things?" Something that Chanel can never be accused of is not using her brain. Her sharp mind is apparent in everything she did, from her savvy use of logos to her deep understanding of the power of personality and packaging, even the importance of being copied. And she was always quotable: "Fashion is not simply a matter of clothes. Fashion is in the air, born upon the wind. One intuits it. It is in the sky and on the road."

Certainly her life was unpredictable. Even her death in 1971, at the age of 87 in her private quarters at the Ritz Hotel — was a plush ending that probably would not have been predicted for Chanel by the nuns in the Aubazine orphanage, where she spent a time as a ward of the state after her mother died and her father ran off. No doubt the sisters at the convent in Moulins, who took her in when she was 17, raised their eyebrows when the young woman left the seamstress job they had helped her get to try for a career as a cabaret singer. This stint as a performer — she was apparently charming but no Piaf — led her to take up with the local swells and become the backup mistress of Etienne Balsan, a playboy who would finance her move to Paris and the opening of her first hat business. That arrangement gave way to a bigger and better deal when she moved on to his friend, Arthur ("Boy") Capel, who is said to have been the love of her life and who backed her expansion from hats to clothes and from Paris to the coastal resorts of Deauville and Biarritz. One of her first successes was the loose-fitting sweater, which she belted and teamed with a skirt. These early victories were similar to the clothes she had been making for herself — women's clothes made out of Everyman materials such as jersey, usually associated with men's undergarments.

It is fitting, somehow, that Chanel was often photographed holding a cigarette or standing in front of her famous Art Deco wall of mirrors. Fashion tends to involve a good dose of smoke and mirrors, so it should come as no surprise that Gabrielle Chanel's version of her life involved a multitude of lies, inventions, cover-ups and revisions. But as Prada said to me: "She was really a genius. It's hard to pin down exactly why, but it has something to do with her wanting to be different and wanting to be independent."

香奈儿：时尚设计者

香奈儿从没有把自己说成是一个女权主义者，而一直强调是女性运动的支持者，事实上，她的工作无疑是女性解放的一部分。她在20世纪20年代和50年代这两个完全不同的年代里，两度将生活女性套装推向市场。她不仅仅关注这些以前只为男性专有的衣物风格，质地和样式，还把这些东西用于自身的穿着上，她把运动衣也视作为时尚语言的一部分。人们可以看到她的风格是如何推动了自然诉求和叛逆的发展。她买不起那个时代的时装，相反她靠产生自己的独特风格而与当时的风尚相左，她就是靠这些原本是男性在运动场上穿着的运动外套和领带，将自己第一次带向社会。

整个20世纪20年代，香奈儿在社交界、女性和时装专业界都取得长足进步，她迅速走向名流。在30年代早期她还在好莱坞受到过关注，可是后来她又回到欧洲。她几乎要和当时欧洲顶级富豪——威斯特敏斯特公爵结婚，然而却最终没能举行婚礼，在解释这个事情时，她说："世上有几个威斯特敏斯特公爵夫人，却只有一个香奈儿。"可是可可·香奈儿也有许多不同面孔，就像她在不同的阶段有着不同的风格一样。其中这些代表作品包括吉普赛短裙，顶级的珠宝饰品的赝品，以及缀满闪烁水晶珠子的黑白乔其纱晚礼服，还有羊毛套装和“小黑裙”。然而要说什么单一作品使得人们记住香奈儿的名字的话，那绝不是这些服装，而是这个液体黄金——装在艺术装饰瓶里的香奈儿5号香水。这是首个用设计者命名的香水。

在20世纪60年代后期，香奈儿也成了她曾经极力抨击和憎恶的“权势集团”的一部分。但如果你观看那个时期的有关她的资料片，依然能够感受到这个泼辣乡妇的尖酸。就是她，把反抗主流时尚界的革命目标锁定在头部——用帽子开创了这一切。她的男孩化的“轻佻女郎”创意与当时流行的古典优雅的帽子风格完全相悖。对于那些流行款式，她说：“一个大脑怎么会在这些东西下面得以运转呢？”香奈儿可永远不会受到不用脑子的指责。她敏锐的思维体现在她所有的创作中，从对商标的机智的使用，到对个性力量，包装魅力，甚至对产品复制的重要性，她都有自己深刻的理解。她总是这样总结说：“时尚不只是衣着，时尚发源于风中，飘逸在空中，人们靠直觉感受，它会出现在天空里也会出现在马路上。”

当然，她的生活同样不可预测。在她母亲死去，父亲不露面的日子里，和她在奥巴钦孤儿院一起生活过的修女们，恐怕无法预测到香奈儿会有这样一个舒服的人生结束方式，1971年，87岁的她死于里兹酒店的私人包房里。当她在年轻时为了当一名夜总会的歌手而放弃了那份穆兰修道院的修女们帮她找的裁缝工作后，毫无疑问，那些在她17岁时把她带入修道院的修女们都感到惊讶。在当歌手的这段期间里她开始明显显露迷人的一面，虽然没有皮雅芙（法国歌手）的实力，但这已经可以让她与地方头面人物开始交往，并且成为艾提安·巴勒松的情妇，就是这位花花公子资助她去巴黎并且开始她第一单帽子生意。在她遇见自己的一生至爱阿瑟·卡伯（男孩）后，沿着这样的道路她越做越好，卡伯资助她的事业从帽子扩大到衣服，从巴黎来到多维耶和比亚里茨的海边度假胜地。她第一个成功之款式是宽松合身毛衣用腰带和裙子搭配。这些早期成功的样式与她做给自己的衣服很相像，即女式服装取材自男士的服装面料，如以前常使用与男性的针织内衣搭配。

无论如何，香奈儿的那些总是拿着烟或是站在她有名的艺术玻璃幕墙前的照片还是挺反映她的真实。时尚就像一缕轻烟和镜面，我们也就毫不意外地会发现，香奈儿的生活观充满大量谎言、发明、包装和变化。但就像蒲如达告诉我说的那样："她真是个天才。虽然很难说清楚为什么，但她总是有着与众不同的东西和独立的个性。"

（孙尚奇　译）

III 政治家

Politicians

The Sons of William the Conqueror

There was once a great king of England who was called William the Conqueror, and he had three sons.

One day King William seemed to be thinking of something that made him very sad; and the wise men who were about him asked him what was the matter.

"I am thinking," he said, "of what my sons may do after I am dead. I am at a loss to know which one of the three ought to be the king when I am gone."

"O king!" said the wise men, "if we only knew what things your sons admire the most, we might then be able to tell what kind of men they will be. Perhaps, by asking them a few questions, we can find out which one of them will be best fitted to rule in your place."

"The plan is well worth trying at least." said the king.

The wise men decided that the young princes should be brought in, one at a time, and that the same questions should be put to each.

"Fair sir," asked one of the wise men, "answer me this question: If, instead of being a boy, it would please God that you should be a bird, what kind of bird would you rather be?"

"A hawk," answered Robert. "I would rather be a hawk, for no other bird reminds one so much of a bold and gallant knight."

"An eagle," answered William. "I would rather be an eagle, because it is strong and brave. It is feared by all other birds, and therefore the king of them all."

"A starling" answered Henry, the youngest brother. "I would rather be a starling, because it is good-mannered and kind and a joy to every one who sees it, and it never tries to rob or abuse its neighbour."

After asking some questions of the sons of William the Conqueror, the wise men talked with one another for a little while, and when they had agreed among themselves, they spoke to the king.

"We find," said the wise men to the king, "that Robert will be bold and gallant. He will do some great deeds, and make a name for himself; but in the end he will be overcome by his foes, and will die in prison. William will be as brave and as strong as the eagle; but he will be feared and hated for his cruel deeds. He will lead a wicked life, and will die a shameful death. Henry will be wise and prudent and peaceful. He will go to war only when he is forced to do so by his enemies. He will be loved at home, and respected abroad; and he will die in peace after having gained great possessions."

Years passed by, and when King William lay upon his deathbed, he declared that Robert should have the lands which he held in France, that William should be the king of England, and that Henry should have no land at all, but only a chest of gold.

So it happened in the end very much as the wise men had foretold. Robert was bold and reckless. He lost all the lands that his father had left him, and was at last shut up in prison, where he was kept until he died. William was so overbearing and cruel that he was feared and hated by all his people. He led a wicked life, and was killed by one of his own men while hunting in the forest.

And Henry had not only the chest of gold for his own, but he became by and by the King of England and the ruler of all the lands that his father had had in France.

征服者威廉的儿子们

从前,英格兰有一位伟大的国王,人们称他为征服者威廉。他有三个儿子。

有一天,威廉国王忧心忡忡,好像在思索什么,他周围的贤士们便问他究竟怎么了。

"我在想,"他说,"我死了以后,我的儿子们会干些什么,我无法断定,他们三个人中哪一个应该继承王位。"

"噢,陛下!"贤士们说,"只要事先知道您的儿子们最喜欢什么,我们就能够说出他们将来会成为什么样的人。或许向他们提几个问题,我们就能够看出哪一个最适合接替你统治国家。"

"这个计策至少很值得一试。"国王说。

贤士们决定把年轻的王子们请来,每次只请一个,并问他们相同的问题。

"殿下,"一个贤士问,"请回答我一个问题:假如上帝不让你做男孩子,而要让你做一只鸟,你会愿意做哪种鸟呢?"

"一只隼,"罗伯特回答说,"我愿意做一只隼,因为其他任何鸟都不能像它那样使人一下子联想到勇猛的骑士。"

"一只鹰,"威廉回答说,"我愿意做一只鹰,因为它强健而勇敢，它是鸟中之王，因此其他鸟都怕它。”

“一只欧椋鸟，”最年轻的亨利回答说，“我愿意做一只欧椋鸟，因为它彬彬有礼而又和蔼可亲，谁看见它都会感到高兴，而且它从来不掠夺或欺负它的邻居。”

在问了征服者威廉的儿子们几个问题之后，这些贤士们互相交谈了一会儿。他们统一了意见之后，就去向国王报告。

“我们发现，”贤士们对国王说，“罗伯特将成为一个大胆而英勇的人。他将做出一些伟大的事业，扬名于天下。但是最后他会被敌人打败，并死在监狱里。威廉将成为一个像雄鹰一样勇敢而强健的人，但他的残暴行为将引起人们的恐惧和憎恨。他会过着一种邪恶的生活，最后将可耻地死去。而亨利将成为一个聪明、谨慎而又温和的人，他只有在迫不得已的情况下才会和敌人作战。他将受到国人的爱戴和外国人的尊敬，并在获得巨大的财富之后寿终正寝。”

多年后，当国王威廉临终时，他宣布罗伯特将继承他在法国的领土，威廉将成为英格兰国王，而亨利却没有得到一点土地，只得到了一箱金子。

最后的结局和贤士们所预言的非常相似。罗伯特胆大而鲁莽，他丢掉了父亲留给他的全部领地，最后被关进监狱，一直到他死去。威廉非常专横而粗暴，他的所有臣民都很怕他、恨他。他过着一种邪恶的生活，最后在一次森林狩猎时被他自己的一个部下杀死。

而亨利不仅仅拥有自己的那一箱金子,不久以后他成为英格兰和他父亲在法国的全部领土的统治者。

Anecdotes of Lincoln

Honest Abe

When Abraham Lincoln was young he worked in a store. As a clerk he proved honest and efficient. One day a woman came into the store and purchased sundry articles. They added up to two dollars and six cents, or the young clerk thought they did. The bill was paid, and the woman was entirely satisfied. But the young store-keeper, not feeling quite sure as to the accuracy of his calculation, added up the items once more. To his dismay he found the sum total should have been but two dollars. "I'ye made her pay six cents too much," said Abraham, disturbed. It was a trifle, and many clerks would have dismissed it as such. But Abraham was too conscientious to forget about the over charge.

"The money must be paid back," he decided. This would have been easy enough had the woman lived just round the corner, but, as the young man knew, she lived between two and three miles away. This, however, did not alter the matter. It was night, but he closed and locked the store, and walked to the residence of his customer. Having arrived there, he explained the matter, paid over the six cents, and returned satisfied.

Am I Uglier Than You?

Abraham Lincoln's ability to laugh at himself sustained him through his many adversities. On example he often recalled was the time when an ugly thug thrust a revolver in his face. Abe tried to remain calm, asking the man what he wanted. The man replied, holding the gun to Lincoln's head, "Some years ago I swore that if I ever came across an uglier man than myself I'd shoot him on the spot."

Relief crossed Lincoln's craggy countenance and he lost all his tension and anxiety. "Shoot me," he said to the stranger, "for if I am an uglier man than you, I don't want to live."

Lincoln's Beard

Lincoln's face is familiar to people all around the world, at least his face when he was wearing a beard. But he didn't wear a beard until later in his life. When he started out as a judge and then a lawyer, he had two nicknames. The first was

Honest Abe. And there are many stories of his honesty both as a child and as he went on throughout all of his life. His second nickname was Homely Abe. He was not good looking. Then something hap pened in 1860. That year Abe Lincoln was the Republican Party nominee, the man the recently formed Republican Party chose as its candidate for President of the United States.

Just a few weeks before the presidential election, Lincoln received a short letter. It was from a girl who lived in New York State. Her name was Grace Bedell. Grace wrote to Lincoln about his homely face, but in a polite way. This was over a hundred and fifty years ago, so Grace didn't use modern English grammar in her letter. But she did write a very interesting letter. Here are some parts of it:

I am a little girl only 11 *years old, but I want you should be the President of the United States very much so I hope you won't think me very bold to write such a great man as you are . . .*

And then Grace went on,

I have got four brothers and part of them will vote for you anyway, and if you will let your whiskers grow, I will try to get the rest of them to vote for you. You would look a great deal better for your face is so thin. All the ladies like whiskers and they would tease their husbands to vote for you, and then you would be President . . .

Lincoln took Grace Bedell's advice, and over the next two weeks he did not shave. By election day on November 6th of 1860, he already had enough whiskers to make a short beard. And he did get elected. Maybe his new beard had something to do with that. And he did wear the beard for the rest of his life.

林肯轶事三则

诚实的亚伯

年轻的亚伯拉罕·林肯曾经在一家小店工作过，并且在工作中显示了高效和诚实的一面。一天一位妇女来到店铺买一些杂货。它们总计 2 美元 6 美分，确切地说这位年轻的店员是这样算的。账付完后妇女非常满意地离开了。但这位年轻的店员，由于感到对刚才的计算的准确度不放心，于是就把各个项目又加了一遍，让他惊奇地是这个账单总额应该只有 2 美元。“我让她多付了 6 美分。”亚伯拉罕不安地说。这样的小事，许多店员都不会太当回事，但亚伯拉罕却不能忘记多收的钱。

"这些钱必须退回去。"他决定。如果这位妇女就住在附近的话,当然就简单,可年轻人知道她住在两三英里外。可这并没有改变什么。到了晚上,他关了店铺,向这位顾客的住地走去。到了那里,他解释了事情,还了 6 美分,满意地回去了。

我比你还丑?

亚伯拉罕·林肯自嘲的能力让他克服了许多难关。他经常回忆的一件事情是,有一次一个丑陋的坏蛋用枪指着他的脸,亚伯尽可能地保持镇静,问那人想要什么。那人用枪对着林肯的头回答道:"几年前我发誓如果我遇到一个比我还难看的人,我就当场杀了他。"

一丝轻松掠过林肯粗糙的脸庞,他的紧张和焦虑解除了。"对我射击,"他对这个陌生人说,"因为如果我比你还丑陋,我也不想活了。"

林肯的大胡子

林肯的那张脸,至少他留着大胡子的脸为世人所熟悉。可是他的胡子是在他后来的日子里才留起来的。在他开始法官,继而是律师的生涯后,他有两个雅号:一个是诚实的亚伯,有许多关于林肯小时候以及以后一生中诚实的故事。另外一个就是其貌不扬的亚伯。他长相不好。可在 1860 年发生了一件事情,当时亚伯·林肯成为共和党的提名人,就是说他被共和党选出作为美国总统的候选人。

就在总统选举前几周，林肯收到了一封短信。它出自纽约的一个小姑娘，格瑞斯·柏黛儿之手。格瑞斯谈到了他那张其貌不扬的脸，当然用语还是挺礼貌的。这事发生在150年前，她的信里也就不是现代的英语语法，但她确实写了一封有趣的信，这里是其中的几段：

我是个只有11岁的小女孩，可我非常想让你成为美国总统，所以我希望你不会因为给你这样的大人物写信而认为我有些鲁莽……

然后，格瑞斯接着写道：

我有四个兄弟，他们其中的几个肯定会选你，如果你让你的胡子长起来的话，我会来说服其他几个也选你。由于你太瘦了，这样的话就会好看得多。女士都喜欢胡子，她们也就会要她们的丈夫也投你的票，这样你就能成为总统了……

林肯采纳了格瑞斯·柏黛儿的建议，后两周他一直留着胡子。在1860年11月6日那个选举日，他已经有足够的胡须成为短髯了，并且他确实选上了。也许他的新胡子真的帮了些忙。在日后的生活里，他一直留着胡子。

（孙尚奇　译）

Stories of Franklin

Hankering for the Sea

Benjamin Franklin was the youngest son among the seventeen children of Josiah Franklin, a candle maker. The whole family worked in the little shop, making candles from the fat of sheep.

Young Franklin did not like the smell of candles and, when no one was watching, often left shop to go down to the harbor. Because Boston was the largest port in the American colonies, young Ben was able to see ships from every nation. He tells us in one of his later writings that he had "a hankering for the sea." If his father had allowed it, he would have left Boston and become a sailor. Josiah Franklin grew very angry with this troublesome son. He refused to let him go to sea, but he gave him his choice between making candles and working in the shop of his brother James, a printer. Ben chose printing and signed a paper that required him to work for his brother until he had reached the age of twenty-two.

Benjamin Franklin, Mrs. Dogood?

In 1721, James Franklin (brother of Benjamin Franklin) began to publish a newspaper, the *New England Courant*. Ben had taught himself to write well by reading good authors. He would put down his own thoughts, copying the style of a famous writer, and then would read the author's book again to see how exact his imitation was. He began to write for the Courant, pretending to be an old woman called "Silence Dogood". James printed letters from Mrs. Dogood in the Courant during the spring and summer of 1722. These letters made fun of various people and things in Boston, and because of them James was put in prison. Even though he would not tell the authorities who had written the letters, James was released. Because Ben was afraid of being named as the author of the offensive letters, he decided to leave Boston.

Strange and Awkward Benjamin

Benjamin Franklin left Boston and went to New York. In those days, New York was such a small city that it did not have a newspaper. In fact, there was only one printer. When Benjamin asked him for a job, ha said he did not need help and advised Ben to go on to Philadelphia, the largest city in the colonies at that time. Ben arrived at Philadelphia with very little money. The first thing he did was to buy three large loaves of bread. He put two of the loaves under his arms, and ate the other one, walking up the main street of Philadelphia and looking at all the buildings and people. A young woman who saw how strange and awkward he looked laughed at him. Ben remembered this meeting all his life; Deborah Read, the young woman, later became Mrs. Benjamin Franklin.

"The Leather Apron"

Benjamin Franklin became the best printer in Philadelphia soon after he arrived there. During his free time, he organized a club. Most of the members were workers, and the club was named for their working clothes, "The Leather Apron".

The members met every Friday evening and talked about science, politics, literature, and philosophy. At the end of each meeting the members decided what they would discuss the following week in order to be able to prepare by reading about the chosen subject. Benjamin proposed that "The Leather Apron" establish a public library to which people could belong by paying a small amount every month for the use of the library room and new books. This was the first public library in America.

Franklin and *Poor Richard's Almanacs*

Ben Franklin began to publish almanacs in 1732. He pretended that they had been written by a person called Richard Saunders. "Poor Richard", as Franklin called him, and his almanacs soon were known all over the colonies. These little pamphlets have been translated into almost every known language.

Why was *Poor Richard's Almanacs* so popular? First, Franklin was a scientist, and every thing he printed about the stars and planets was correct. In addition to dependable information, there were pieces of verse and many short, wise sayings. Poor Richard believed that people should work hard, save their money, live simply, and be honest. In all sorts of ways he taught the people of all the colonies that the way to build a prosperous country was to be absolutely honest and thorough in whatever they did. Here are some pieces of advice from *Poor Richard's Almanacs:*

A word to the wise is sufficient.

The used key is always bright.

If you love life, do not waste time, for that's what life is made of.

One today is worth two tomorrows.

Keep your shop and your shop will keep you.

If you would have a faithful servant, and one that you like, serve yourself.

A small leak will sink a great ship.

If you would know the value of money, go and try to borrow some.

Experience keeps a dear school, but fools will learn in no other.

Early to bed and early to rise makes a man healthy, wealthy, and wise.

Franklin's Kite

The story of Benjamin Franklin's kite is known everywhere. He had been experimenting with electricity, and in 1751 had published a paper saying that electricity and lightning were the same thing. Both were bright, both were the same yellow color, both made a noise, both made crooked flashes, and both would pass through metal.

In order to test his claim, he and his son took a kite made of silk (because it is stronger than paper), and added a long wire to the top and a piece of silk to the end of the string with which he controlled the kite. A metal key was hung where the silk and string met. They flew the kite up into a thunderstorm, keeping themselves dry under a roof. When the kite reached the storm clouds, Franklin noticed that all the loose parts of his string began to stand up and shake. When the kite touched lightning, a spark ran down the string to the key; a rush of electric sparks began to appear on the key. As the string became wetter, the sparks came faster. They were sparks of electricity. Lightning was in deed electricity.

Franklin decided to use this knowledge in a practical way. He invented the lightning rod. Ladies in Europe took to wearing lightning rods on their hats and trailing a ground wire — a fad that began after Benjamin Franklin published instructions on how to make them, in his almanac, *Poor Richard Improved,* in 1753.

富兰克林的故事

渴望当水手

蜡烛制造商乔塞艾·富兰克林有十七个孩子，本杰明·富兰克林是最小的一个。富兰克林全家都在这个小店里干活，他们用羊脂制作蜡烛。

年轻的富兰克林不喜欢蜡烛的气味，在没人盯着的时候，他就离开店铺，跑到港口去。波士顿是当时的英国在美洲殖民地最大的港口，所以年轻人可以看到来自世界各地的船只，他在后来的文章中提到过他曾经“向往大海”。要是他父亲当时同意的话，他就离开波士顿而成为一名水手了。乔塞艾·富兰克林对这个不断惹麻烦的儿子越来越生气，他拒绝了儿子当水手的请求，告诉他要么做蜡烛，要么在做印刷的詹姆斯哥哥的店里干活。本杰明选择了后者并为此签了一份合约：22 岁前他都要在哥哥那里干。

富兰克林，杜古德夫人？

1721 年，哥哥詹姆斯·富兰克林开始出版一份报纸，叫《新英格兰报》。本杰明通过阅读优秀作者的文章而在写作上自学成才。他会照着一个著名的作家的风格写一些表达自己思想的文章，然后再读一遍原作，来确认自己模仿的程度。他开始以“沉默的杜古德”夫人的名义为这家报纸投稿，在 1722 年春夏期间，哥哥詹姆斯在报纸上刊登了杜古德夫人的来信。这些来信对波士顿的各方人士和事件都进行了嘲讽，为此詹姆斯被抓了起来，虽然哥哥没有把作者的真实姓名告诉当局，他还是被释放了。由于本杰明害怕有人指认自己是真正的作者，他决定离开波士顿。

奇怪而笨拙的本杰明

本杰明·富兰克林离开波士顿后来到了纽约。在那个年代纽约还是个没有自己报纸的小城市。连印刷商也只有一位。本杰明希望能在他的手下干活，由于这里并不缺人手，他建议本杰明到当时殖民地区域内最大的城市——费城。本杰明到达费城时已经几乎手无分文，他首先买了三只面包，把两只夹在腋下，边吃着第三只面包，他沿着费城的主干道一路观看着建筑和人群。一位青年女性看着他这副奇异的样子不由得笑了起来。本杰明一辈子都记着这次碰面，那位年轻小姐黛博拉·里德，后来成为了本杰明夫人。

"皮围裙"

在他到达费城后不久，本杰明就成为这里顶级印刷工。在空闲时间，他组织了一个俱乐部，其中多数的成员是工人，俱乐部的名字也是他们工装的名字："皮围裙"。

成员们每周五聚到一起，谈论科学、政治、文学和哲学。到结束时他们还会决定下一周的讨论议题，这样他们就可以事先去阅读这方面的文章。本杰明建议"皮围裙"建立一个公共图书馆，这样他们就可以只要每月付少量的费用就能使用图书馆的房间并阅读新书。这是美国历史上第一个公共图书馆。

富兰克林与《可怜的理查德历书》

在1732年，本杰明开始出版历书，他号称这些是由一名叫理查德·桑德斯的人写的。本杰明称呼他为"可怜的理查德"。这些书籍很快在殖民地有了名气。这些小册子几乎被翻译成了所有的文字。

为什么《可怜的理查德历书》会流行呢？首先富兰克林是个科学家，他关于恒星和行星的文章都非常正确，除了这些可信的信息外，书中还有许多诗句和简短的名言。“可怜的理查德”相信人们应该努力工作，储存资金，简单生活，诚实可信。他用各种方法让殖民地的人们知道要建立一个有前景的国家，人民就要绝对诚实和持之以恒。这里引用的就是《可怜的理查德》中的几点建议：

聪明人，一句话就足矣。

用过的钥匙总是管用。

热爱生命，就不要浪费时间，因为生命由时间组成。

今日的价值两倍于明天。

你有店铺，则店铺会维持你的生活。

如果想有一个忠诚而又令人喜欢的仆人，那就自己来做吧。

小裂缝沉大船。

要知道钱的价值，去试着问别人借借看。

经验即学校，但愚者却不知。

早睡早起，使人健康、富裕和聪明。

富兰克林的风筝

本杰明·富兰克林的风筝故事到处传扬。他一直在进行有关电动试验研究，到了1751年，他在一篇研究报告中指出电和雷电是同一样东西，都具有明亮性质，相同的黄光，都会发出巨响，都会产生弯曲的闪光以及同样可以通过金属体。

为了证实他的主张，他和他的儿子拿了用丝质的风筝（比纸结实），在风筝顶端加上了一根长导线，在控制风筝的末端连上一片丝绸，在两者的连接处，还系上了一把金属钥匙。他们把风筝飞入雷雨中，自己则站在屋檐下，避免淋湿。当风筝接触到雷雨云时，他注意到绳子的松弛垂下部分开始立了起来并且开始摆动。当风筝碰到闪电时，一个火花沿着绳子奔向那把钥匙，接着一串电火花出现在钥匙上，绳子越来越湿，火花也就越来越快。他们是电火花。闪电就是电。

富兰克林决定把这个知识进入一个实际操作中，他发明了避雷针。欧洲的女士们开始在帽子上装一个避雷针，还有一根接地线。这是当时的一种风尚，而这一切都因富兰克林1753年在他的历书《可怜的理查德升级版》中介绍如何制作避雷针而起。

Jefferson: Make No Promises For the Presidency

While the Presidential election was taking place in the House of Representatives, amid scenes of great excitement, strife and intrigue, which was to decide whether Jefferson or Burr should be the chief magistrate of the nation, Jefferson was stopped one day, as he was coming out of the Senate chamber, by Governor Morris, a prominent leader of the Federalists.

Mr. Morris said, "I wish to have an earnest talk with you, Mr. Jefferson, on the alarming situation of things."

"I am very glad," said Jefferson, "to talk matters over with you."

"As you well know," said Mr. Morris, "I have been strenuously opposing you, as have also the large majority of the States."

"To be frank with you," he continued, "we are very much afraid of you. We fear, first, that you will turn all the

Federalists out of office; second, that you will put down the navy; third, that you will wipe off the public debt. Now, if you will declare, or authorize your friends to declare that you will not take these steps, your election will be made sure."

Mr. Jefferson replied, "Governor Morris, I naturally want to be President, and yet I cannot make any terms to obtain the position. I shall never go into the office by capitulation. I cannot have my hands tied by any conditions which would hinder me from pursuing the measures which I deem best for the public good. I must be perfectly free. The world can judge my future course by that which I have hitherto followed. I am thankful to you for your interest, but I cannot make the slightest promise."

杰斐逊：不为当选总统而作任何承诺

当众议院正在进行总统选举时，为了决定到底是杰斐逊还是伯尔将成为国家总统，发生了一幕幕异常激烈而又充满斗争和阴谋的场景。一天正当杰斐逊走出参议院时，北部联邦同盟的著名领导人莫里斯州长叫住了他。

莫里斯说："杰斐逊先生，我想就目前令人担忧的形势和你诚恳地交谈一次。”

杰斐逊说：“我非常愿意和你讨论这些问题。”

“正如你所熟知的那样，”莫里斯说，“我一直都在坚决地反对你，就像我们州里绝大多数人那样。坦率地说，我们都很怕你。我们担心，第一，你会把所有联邦主义者赶出政府；第二，你会裁减海军；第三，你会勾销公债。现在，如果你宣布，或是授权你的朋友们宣布你将保证不采取这些措施，那么你的当选就能得到保证。”

杰斐逊回答说：“莫里斯州长，我当然很想当总统，但是我不能为获得这一职位而达成任何协议。我永远不会通过投降来进入政府。我的双手不能被任何妨碍我追求那些我认为对公众最有利的措施的条件所束缚。我必须完全自由。世人会通过迄今为止我一直在遵循的事物来判断我将来的路线。我感谢你的好意，但是我不能作丝毫的承诺。”

（逸云　译）

Franklin D. Roosevelt: A Man of Courage

In 1921, Franklin D. Roosevelt took his family sailing one day and he fell overboard into the chilly waters. The next day, a forest fire broke out. Franklin and his children helped to fight the forest fire and put it out. It was hard and tiring work. After the fire was out, Franklin was sick. It was polio. He could not move his legs. The doctors said he could never walk again.

Many men would have given up then. Franklin Roosevelt did not give up. He began to work to get well again. Even though he could not get out of bed, he did exercises, and his shoulders and arms grew very strong. At last the doctors let him out of bed, but he had to wear heavy metal braces on his legs. Then he went to Warm Springs, Georgia. He swam in the warm waters there. Even though it was painful to move his legs, he kept on swimming and exercising them. He grew better until he could leave the braces off. He could walk with only a cane to help him.

"The only thing we have to fear is fear itself," President Roosevelt told the people.

富兰克林·D.罗斯福：一个有勇气的人

1921年某天，在富兰克林·D.罗斯福带了家人乘船游览的时候，他跌进了寒冷刺骨的河水里。翌日，有个森林发生火灾，富兰克林和他的孩子们帮助扑灭了大火。那真是又艰苦又劳累的工作。大火扑灭后，富兰克林得了麻痹症。他不能挪动双腿。医生们说他永远不能再行走了。

许多人要是患了这种病就会觉得失望。可是富兰克林·罗斯福却毫不灰心。他开始活动来争取恢复健康。虽然他不能起床，可他还是锻炼，使肩膀和手臂长得很结实。最后医生们同意他起床，但是他还得在腿上戴着沉重的金属支撑。他于是到佐治亚州温泉去，在温水里游泳。虽然活动双腿十分疼痛，他还是坚持游泳和锻炼。他逐渐痊愈，终于不再需用支撑，仅仅借助一根手杖便能行走了。

罗斯福总统对人民说："可惧者莫甚于畏惧。"

Winston Churchill: His Other Life

Winston Churchill began his interest in painting in his 40s. As First Lord of the Admiralty in 1915, he was deeply *involved* in a campaign in the Dardanelles that could have shortened the war. But when the mission failed, he paid the price. He was removed from the admiralty.

"I thought he would die of grief." said his wife. But he took his home to a farm. There, as Churchill later remembered, "The painting saved me!"

Walking in the garden one day, he happened to see his sister in law painting with watercolors. He watched her for a few minutes, then borrowed her brush and tried his hand.

Churchill soon decided to experiment with brushes. Glad to see him free from his dark days, his wife rushed to buy whatever she could find. He started with the sky and later described how "very careful I mixed a little blue paint on the palette, and then made a mark as big as a bean on the snow-white board."

At that time, John Lavery — a Churchill neighbor and famous painter was teaching him in his art. Later, Lavery said of his student: "If he had chosen painting instead of a politician, I believe he would be a great master with the brush."

In painting, Churchill had found a companion with whom he was to walk for the greater part of the years that remained to him. After the war, in 1921, the death of his mother was followed later by the loss of his lovely daughter, Marigold. Churchill was very sad, and he found the comfort in his painting. He wrote to his wife: "I went out and painted a beautiful river in the afternoon, light and golden hills in the background. But I kept feeling the hurt of Marigold."

Historians have called the ten years after 1929, when the Conservative government fell and Winston was out of the office, his wilderness years. But during the ten years, he often painted in the South of France. Of the 500 pictures he left, 250 dated from 1930 to 1939.

Painting was a joy to Churchill to the end of his life. He had written in his book *Painting as a Pastime*, "Light and color, peace and hope, will keep them company to the end of the day."

温斯顿·丘吉尔：生活侧记

温斯顿·丘吉尔在四十多岁时迷恋上绘画。那是在1915年，任海军大臣的他，积极投身于在达达尼尔海峡的一场战役中，这场战役本可以缩短世界大战。但由于遭受失败，丘吉尔付出了代价，他被调离出海军部。

他的妻子说："我想他会痛苦而死。"但他携家带口来到了一个农场，在那儿，丘吉尔后来回忆到："是绘画拯救了我！"

一天，他在花园散步时，偶然看见他的弟媳在用水彩作画。他观察了几分钟，然后向她借了画笔并一试身手。

丘吉尔很快就决定试试去画画。看到他从阴暗的忧思中解脱出来，他的妻子非常开心，她赶快去买所有能买到的颜料。他先从天空画起，后来他描述如何"非常谨慎地在调色板上加入一点蓝色调，在这块雪白的板上点上豌豆大的一笔"。

那时，约翰·拉威利——丘吉尔的邻居，也是一位有名的画家——正教丘吉尔学画。后来提及他的这位特殊的学生，拉威利说："倘若他选择绘画而不是从政，我相信他会是位绘画大师的。"

在绘画中，丘吉尔找到了能陪他度过余生大部分时光的知己。战后，在1921年，母亲刚刚去世两个月，他就失去了他深爱着的3岁女儿玛丽戈尔德。这时绘画给了他一些安慰。丘吉尔非常悲伤，于是他就用绘画来解脱自己。他在给妻子的信中说："我出外画了一条夕阳下美丽的溪流，背后映着晚霞的群山。但我失去玛丽戈尔德的痛苦总是挥之不去。"

史学家把1929年后的十年，也就是保守党垮台的时间，称为他的"荒凉岁月"。但这些年间他经常在法国南部作画。在现存的500多幅油画中，大约250幅是他在1930年至1939年间的作品。

绘画给丘吉尔带来的乐趣直至他人生的尽头。在他所著的《画中的消遣》里说，"光与色，和平与希望，会始终伴随着人们。"

Margaret Thatcher: The Iron Lady Sobbed

In 1982, Mark Thatcher, the son of Mrs. Thatcher, was reported missing in the Sahara Desert while competing in the Motor Race from Paris to Dakar. This sad news shook the usually calm politician. Though she did her best to pretend as if nothing had happened and made her appearances as usual, people could not fail to notice that she was no longer the old self-assured prime minister who always had everything under control. Instead, she had become a very sad mother who was unable to recover from her shock.

One day, when she was to speak at a luncheon party, a reporter caught her by bringing up the subject of her missing son again. She was totally unprepared for the question and lost her self-control. Tears were rolling from her eyes as she sobbingly told the reporter that there was still no news of Mark and that she was very worried about him. She said that some countries had promised to do their best to help her find her son. With that she broke down completely and sobbed silently for quite a while. Gradually she calmed down and started to speak as planned. It was a very moving scene which showed a new side of Mrs. Thatcher's character the public did not usually see, so people began to talk about the Iron lady's maternal love, which is very universal to all human kind.

Later Mark returned safe and sound to his mother's side, and smiled as usual, as if nothing unusual had ever happened. The Iron lady, however, broke down again and was seen sobbing for the second time.

玛格丽特·撒切尔：铁娘子流泪了

据报道，1982 年撒切尔夫人的儿子——马克·撒切尔参加由巴黎至达喀尔的摩托车赛时，在撒哈拉沙漠失踪了。这则意想不到的消息震惊了这位一向镇定自如的政治家。尽管她尽力装出什么也没发生，跟平时一样，在公开的场合抛头露面，但是人们不能不注意到她不再是昔日那个能掌控一切的首相了。相反，她成为一位无法从这一打击中恢复过来的悲伤母亲。

有一天，她要在午宴上发言，一个记者乘她不备又提出了有关她儿子失踪的话题。对此，撒切尔夫人在精神上完全没有准备，结果失去了自我控制，眼泪夺眶而出。她向这位记者哭诉依然没有马克的消息，她非常为他担忧。她说一些国家向她承诺竭尽全力帮她找回儿子。说完以后她完全不能自制了，默默地呜咽了很长一段时间。她渐渐地镇静下来，开始按原计划发言。这是一个非常动人的场面，展示了公众通常看不到的撒切尔夫人性格新的一面，于是人们开始谈论起铁娘子的母爱——一种全人类普遍的感情。

后来马克安然无恙地回到了他母亲的身边，如以往一样心情愉快，笑容满面，好像没有什么异乎寻常的事发生过。然而，铁娘子又一次不能自制，第二次被人看见流泪了。

Martin Luther King, Jr.: One of the Most Extraordinary Humans

Martin Luther King, Jr. was more than just an inspirational black leader. His desire and ability to rise above his own failings and those of fellow humans uplifted us all — both those who were living at the time and those who have come after. Even if we do not know it, our world is a better place because of his light.

Dr. King's life was extinguished more than 30 years ago, but not his light. It is still here for each of us to carry, and to illuminate even brighter with our own unique creativity and contribution.

Martin Luther King, Jr. was born on January 15, 1929 in Atlanta, Georgia. After graduating from Morehouse College and becoming a minister, he made his way to Montgomery, Alabama in 1954. This was an important decision for it was in the same city that, on December 1 of the following year, Rosa

Parks refused to give up her bus seat to a white man. King was elected president of the Montgomery Improvement Association and led a boycott of. Montgomery buses throughout 1956, which brought him national recognition.

King's legacy of non-violent activism was influenced by the teachings of Jesus and Gandhi. King reinforced and expanded his Biblical convictions during a visit to India in 1959, where he studied Gandhi's methods of non-violent protest. The knowledge was put to effective use through non-violent civil rights protests during the early 1960's.

A gifted orator, King ignited the world and a generation in the cause for American civil rights with his *I Have a Dream* speech on Aug 28, 1963 to a crowd of 250, 000 in Washington, D. C.

"We must forever conduct our struggle on the high plan of dignity and discipline. We must not allow our creative protests to degenerate into physical violence. Again and again we must rise to the majestic heights of meeting physical force with soul force. ... I have a dream that one day this nation will rise up and live out the true meaning of its creed: We hold these truths to be self-evident: that all men are created equal. ... When we let freedom ring, when we let it ring from every village and every hamlet, from every state and every city, we will be able to speed up that day when all of God's children, black men and white men, Jews and Gentiles, Protestants and Catholics, will be able to join hands and sing in the words of the old Negro spiritual, 'Free at last! Free at last! Thank God Almighty, we are free at last!'"

Dr. King received the Nobel Peace Prize and was named *Time Magazine*'s "Person of the Year" in 1964. In his Nobel Prize acceptance speech, he said, "Non-violence is the answer to the crucial political and moral questions of our time: the need for man to overcome oppression and violence without resorting to oppression and violence. Man must evolve for all human conflicts a method which rejects revenge, aggression and retaliation. The foundation of such a method is love."

King was one of the most extraordinary humans to ever grace our planet. He was a man who met hate and hopelessness with love and inspiration. He used non-violence to point out the obscenity of violence.

马丁·路德·金:最非凡的伟人之一

马丁·路德·金不仅仅是一个充满激情的黑人领袖,他和同伴虽然有过多次失败,但他却渴望并能够重新站立起来,这鼓舞着我们所有的人——包括与他同时代的人,也包括后来的人。即便我们并不知道这一点,但我们的世界确实在他的光芒照耀下变得更加美好。

金博士的生命在三十多年前就结束了,但他的光芒并未消失。现在它仍需要我们大家去继承发扬,用我们非凡的创造力和奉献精神使它更为灿烂夺目。

马丁·路德·金于1929年1月5日出生在佐治亚州亚特兰大市。从莫尔豪斯学院毕业后,他当了牧师,并于1954年前往阿拉巴马州蒙哥马利市。这是一个非常重要的决定,因为第二年的12月1日,就是在这座城市,发生了罗莎·帕克斯在公共汽车上拒绝把座位让给一名白人男子的事情。金当选为蒙哥马利进步联盟的主席,并在1956年长达一年的时间里,领导了联合抵制蒙哥马利公共汽车的运动。这件事使他闻名全国。

金留给我们的非暴力行动主义是在耶稣的教义和甘地的思想影响下形成的。1959年在印度期间,金研究了甘地的非暴力抵抗的方法，这进一步强化并扩展了他对基督教义的坚定信念。在20世纪60年代早期的非暴力民权抗议运动中，他成功运用了这一理念。

金是一位天才演说家。1963年8月28日，他在华盛顿特区面对25万民众发表的《我有一个梦》的演说，激励了全世界和为美国民权事业奋斗的一代人。

“我们必须永远坚持在保持尊严和严守纪律的高度开展斗争，我们一定不能使富有创造性的抗争沦为身体暴力，我们必须努力不懈地升华到以心灵力量来对付肉体力量的神圣境界。……我有一个梦，有一天，这个国家将站起来，并实现其信条的真正含义：所有的人生来都是平等的。……当我们让自由之声响彻之时，当我们让它从每一座村落，从每一个州和每一座城市响起时，我们将能加速这一天的到来，那时上帝的所有孩子们，黑人和白人、犹太人和非犹太人、基督徒和天主教徒们将手挽手，高唱那古老的黑人圣歌‘终于自由了！终于自由了！感谢全能的上帝，我们终于自由了！’”

1964年，金博士获得了诺贝尔和平奖，并被《时代》杂志评为“年度风云人物”。在诺贝尔的授奖演说中，他说道，“非暴力是我们这个时代最关键的政治和道德总的解决方法：人类不需要使用压迫和暴力来对付压迫和暴力。人类一定要为解决人类冲突衍生一种方法，这一方法拒绝报复、侵犯和仇杀。这一方法的根基就是爱。”

金是一位为我们这个星球增添光彩、最非凡的伟人。他以爱消除恨,以振奋挽救绝望,以非暴力揭示了暴力的丑恶。

Arnold Schwarzenegger: From a Movie Star to the Governor of California

He had a name you couldn't pronounce, an accent you couldn't cut, and a body out of a Frank Frazetta painting, yet this world champion bodybuilder defied all the naysayers to become the undisputed biggest movie star in the World, as well as a restaurateur, political activist, leading spokesman for physical fitness, and now further — the governor of California.

Arnold Schwarzenegger was born on July 30, 1947 in a small town of Austria. The name Schwarzenegger means "black plowman". His father Gustav was a former military officer who later became a policeman and his mother was a housewife. They all lived above the police station, where Gustav worked.

After seeing the Olympic swim champion Johnny

Weissmüller in Graz, Arnold was so inspired by Johnny's physique that he decided he wanted to become a champion athlete and started training. In the early years Arnold practiced a lot of different sports such as skating, skiing, swimming and table-tennis. Because of the interest in sports the school came in the second place and did not get much attention. Gustav wanted Arnold to become a world-class soccer player, but at the age of thirteen, Arnold dropped out of the soccer team.

He was looking for a role model and found one on the silver screen, Hercules. He watched all the Hercules movies over and over. He started to collect muscle magazines and was so impressed by the strength and the muscles in the magazine that he had just one goal clear in his mind. So he started to train.

By the age of twenty he had been named Mr. Germany and runner up in his first Mr. Universe. When he retired in 1975 he had been awarded Mr. Universe five times, Mr. Olympia six times and Mr. World once. But five years after his retirement in 1980 he won his seventh Mr. Olympia title.

After conquering the world as the greatest bodybuilder who ever lived, he went to America to make his name in motion pictures. Hampered by his impossible name and thick accent, success eluded him for many years. He first appeared in the low-budget, barely released *Hercules in New York*, billed as Arnold Strong. The movie revealed two things: his impressively sculptured body, and the fact that he couldn't act (let alone speak English). Schwarzenegger's film debut sent him back to the weight room, and he concentrated on bodybuilding for some time thereafter, winning seven Mr. Olympia titles — a record only recently beaten — and earning the nickname "the Austrian Oak".

He was then cast as a bodybuilder in the comedy *Stay Hungry*. His performance was, in the main, kindly reviewed, but Schwarzenegger still didn't actively pursue a screen career until accepting the role of the impeccably costumed Handsome Stranger in a cartoonish Western, *The Villain* (1979). He realized that he'd milked body-building and decided to tackle a new career.

Schwarzenegger threw himself wholeheartedly into acting, beginning with roles in *Scavenger Hunt* (1979) and *The Jayne Mansfield Story* (1980) and other movies in the following years, then graduating to the title role of 1982's sword-and-sorcery blockbuster *Conan the Barbarian* and its 1984 sequel, *Conan the Destroyer*. It wasn't until he found this tailor-made role of Conan that he truly came into his own as a performer. A succession of action films made him an international box office star.

Later in 1984 he starred in *The Terminator* that cast him as an unstoppable killer robot from the future; its success made him a superstar and gave him a signature line — "I'll be back!"— that he managed to work into many subsequent films for a knowing laugh. In fact, Schwarzenegger's sense of humor (even about himself) set him apart from the other action stars of the 1980s.

He has solidified his undisputable position as one of the most popular — if not the most popular — movie stars in the world. Besides, in 1990 he was named chairman of the President's Council on Physical Fitness, and his lengthy association with Republican politics sparked rumors at that time that he might someday run for office. Ironically, he is married to a TV journalist Maria Shriver, one of the (Democratic) Kennedy clan. Now the rumors have turned to reality — the former star of strength and movies is smiling to the world in the chair of Governor of California. "I'm here." The household-known screen Terminator says.

阿诺·施瓦辛格：从电影明星到加州州长

他的名字你不会念，他的口音你听不懂，他的躯体仿佛弗兰克·弗拉泽塔笔下的奇幻英雄，这位世界健美冠军在反对声中迎难而上，成为无可争议的世界电影巨星；此外，他还是餐馆老板、政治活动家和健身运动首席代言人。现在，他又多了一重身份——加利福尼亚州的州长。

阿诺·施瓦辛格于1947年7月30日出生在奥地利的一个小镇。他的姓氏“施瓦辛格”意为“黑色庄稼汉”。父亲古斯塔夫曾是位军官，退伍后当了警察，母亲则是家庭主妇。一家人住在古斯塔夫就职的警察局楼上。

在格拉茨见到奥运游泳冠军约翰尼·维斯穆勒之后，阿诺受其体格鼓舞，立志成为运动健将，并且开始了训练。年轻时的阿诺练习过许多不同的体育项目，比如溜冰、滑雪、游泳，和乒乓球。他热衷运动，以至忽略了学业。古斯塔夫想让阿诺成为世界级的足球运动员，但阿诺在13岁那年退出了足球队。

他开始寻找榜样，并在银幕上如愿以偿，大力神海格力斯成了他的偶像。他一遍遍重温所有以海格力斯为主角的电影。他开始收集健美杂志,杂志中表现的力量和肌肉令他折服,一个目标在他脑海中清晰起来。就这样,他开始了训练。

20 岁那年,他获得了"德国先生"的称号,还在"宇宙先生"竞赛中取得亚军。到 1975 年退役时,他已经获得五次"宇宙先生"、六次"奥林匹亚先生"和一次"世界先生"称号。而在退役五年之后的 1980 年,他第七度获颁"奥林匹亚先生"头衔。

阿诺作为史上最伟大的健美运动员征服了世界,随后,他来到美国,希望能在电影界闯出名声。但由于名字拗口、口音浓重,阿诺连续多年未获成功。他先是出演了勉强发行的小成本电影《大力神在纽约》,在片中使用的名字是"阿诺·大壮"。这部电影表现了两样东西:阿诺那雕像一般的身体和他不会演戏(更不会说英语)的事实。电影首映失败,阿诺只得重返健身房,他在此后的一段时间里专心健身,并七次获得"奥林匹亚先生"的称号——这个纪录最近才被打破——人们还亲切地将他称为"奥地利橡树"。

其后,他又在喜剧电影《别吃太饱》中出演健美运动员。人们对他的表演大致予以善意的评价,但施瓦辛格对于电影事业仍旧不大热衷,直到他接拍了卡通式的西部片《疯狂大镖客》(1979 年),并在其中出演衣着考究的英俊陌生人一角。这时,他觉得自己在健美领域已经难以再有作为,于是决定从事新的职业。

施瓦辛格全心投入了演艺事业。他先是在1979年的《遗产大搜索》和1980年的《昙花一现》中扮演角色，接下去几年又出演了其他几部电影，1982年，他晋身主角，在魔幻动作大片《王者之剑》及其续集《毁天灭地》(1984年)中出演主人公柯南。找到了这个度身定做的角色之后，阿诺才成了一名真正的表演者。此后的一系列动作电影使他成为享誉国际的票房巨星。

1984年下半年，他在电影《终结者》中领衔，扮演来自未来的无敌机器杀手；影片的成功使阿诺成为超级巨星，他从此多了句著名的口头禅"我会回来的！"在后来拍摄的许多影片中，他都会说出这句台词，观众听了则发出会意的大笑。事实上，正是施瓦辛格的幽默(甚至不乏自嘲)将他与其他80年代的动作明星区分了开来。

至此，阿诺已奠定了自己无可争议的地位，成为大受世人欢迎的影星——如果不是最受世人欢迎的话。此外，他还在1980年接任总统健身委员会主席，他长期与共和党的政治活动保持联系，人们由此议论纷纷，说他或将竞选公职。但他却和出身民主党人肯尼迪家族的电视记者玛丽娅·史利弗结为夫妇，其中不无反讽意味。现在，传言已经成真，这位昔日的力量与电影之星，眼下正在加州州长的位置上对全世界发出微笑。"我来了。"这位家喻户晓的银幕终结者这样说道。

（高天羽　译）

IV 企业家

Entrepreneurs

John D. Rockefeller

John D. Rockefeller was born in 1839 on a farm near Richford, New York, a small town in the western part of the state. He was a hard-working boy, both in school and outside of school.

Rockefeller began to look for work when he finished high school at age sixteen. Since the age of five, he had worked at odd jobs, such as raising turkeys or working in potato fields. Now he looked for better opportunities.

At first, Rockefeller worked in an office, where he was successful and where he learned a great deal about business. But he wanted to go into business for himself. So he and a friend formed a partnership to buy and sell grain, hay, and other farm products.

The business was successful, but Rockefeller decided to go into the new oil industry. He formed his own company so that he could make free use of his skill and imagination in business.

The company Rockefeller started became the Standard Oil Company. It took the oil from wells and refined it, that is, changed it into products such as kerosene and grease.

Rockefeller's business grew and grew until it was worth millions of dollars. Almost everyone who bought oil products had to buy them from the Standard Oil Company. Finally, the government and the courts ordered the Standard Oil Company to be divided up to give other oil companies a chance.

John D. Rockefeller earned a great fortune and he gave away much money. By the time of his death, Rockefeller had created a special fund of money to be used to improve health and education, and another fund to improve "the well-being of mankind throughout the world." During his lifetime, Rockefeller had gained almost one billion dollars; he gave away about half of it.

约翰·D.洛克菲勒

约翰·D.洛克菲勒在1839年生于纽约州西部一个小镇里奇福德附近的一个农场里。无论在校内或校外，洛克勒菲都是一个勤奋的孩子。

他16岁念完中学就开始找工作做了。从5岁起他曾干过一些零星杂活,如饲养火鸡或在马铃薯田里干活等等。现在他要寻找更好的工作机会。

起初洛克菲勒在一个办公室里工作。在那里他干得挺好,还学到了许多做买卖的本领。可是他要自己做生意,因而他和一个朋友合伙买卖谷物、干草和其他农产品。

买卖非常成功,但是洛克菲勒决定经营新兴的石油工业。他建立了自己的公司,这样他可充分地发挥他的贸易才能和设想了。

洛克菲勒开办的公司是美孚石油公司。它从油井开采石油,加以精炼,成为煤油、润滑油等产品。

洛克菲勒的企业不断扩展,达到价值数百万美元。几乎所有购买石油产品的人都得向美孚石油公司购买。最后,政府和法院命令该公司进行划分,给其他石油公司提供贸易机会。

约翰·D.洛克菲勒发了大财,他也捐赠了许多钱。洛克菲勒在临终前已为促进保健和教育事业创立了一项专门基金,另一项基金用来增进"全世界的幸福"。他一生挣得的财产将近有10亿美元之多,他捐赠了大约一半钱财。

Carnegie's Wealth

Carnegie Earned $1.20 a Week

Andrew Carnegie(1835 -1919, American industrialist and philanthropist) began to work, when he was only twelve years old, as a bobbin boy in a cotton mill. He worked from six in the morning until six at night, putting thread on the bobbins that were used in the weaving machines. He earned 20 cents a day, or $1.20 a week.

Andrew was determined to become something better than a bobbin boy. He worked very hard, and in a few months he was given a new job at $1.65—putting coal into the furnace that provided the steam power for the looms. The work was hard and dangerous because the boiler might explode and kill him if he were not careful, but extra money was needed in the Carnegie home.

Later, Andrew became a messenger boy for $2.50 a week. This was very good pay for a boy of fourteen. He was smaller than the other four messengers, but he was the fastest of all. Soon he was earning $3.00 a week. When he was not running around town with messages, Andrew learned to understand the Morse code. Finally, he studied well enough to become a telegraph operator, earning $25 a month. He was then sixteen years old.

Andrew Carnegie, one of the richest Americans ever, practically became allergic to money as he grew richer and older. He was offended, he said, just by the sight and touch of it, and never carried any. Because he had no money with him with which to pay the fare, Carnegie was once put off a London tram.

His Company Was Valued $500 Million

In 1853, Andrew Carnegie met Thomas Scott, a young superintendent of the Pennsylvania Railroad. The railroad acted on Carnegie's suggestions and did build its own telegraph lines. Scott asked Andrew to operate the new telegraph and to be his assistant in the office. Andrew accepted. The pay was $35.00 a month and besides, it offered Andrew a wonderful opportunity to rise in the world.

In 1862, he organized the Keystone Bridge Company to build the first iron bridge across the Ohio River. In 1873 he established the J. Edgar Thomason Steel Mill.

The new mill was a success from the start. In 16 years more steel was made in the United States than in England, where it had been made so much earlier. In 1888 Andrew Carnegie bought a controlling interest in a company almost as large as his, and in several other steel mills near Pittsburgh. He joined all these different companies into the Carnegie Corporation. This organization included mines, steel mills, ships, and railroad lines to bring material into Pittsburgh from all over the country and to take the finished steel out again. The Carnegie Corporation owned everything needed to make and to distribute steel. In 1901 his company, valued five hundred million dollars, was sold to the United States Steel Corporation, formed by the famous American banker, John Pierpont Morgan. Mr. Morgan then said that Carnegie was "the richest man in the world". He had come from $1.20 a week to this.

What Did He Do with His Money?

Carnegie spent almost twenty years left to him giving his wealth away. He believed that those who became rich should return what they did not need to society. He had said that a rich man "dies disgraced" if he does not use the ability he has shown in gathering money to give away his money for the public good during his lifetime.

He began to use his money to build free public libraries. In 1919 it was said that his money had built almost 3, 000 libraries, valued altogether at over sixty million dollars. Most of these were in the United States, but some of them were in Canada, Great Britain, New Zealand, and even as far as the Fiji Islands.

A gift of four million dollars was made to Carnegie's hometown, Dunfermline, Scotland. It was used to build parks and playgrounds for the people of the town. Pittsburgh, where he made his fortune, was given a music hall, a museum, an art gallery, and a public library.

Andrew Carnegie's public gifts amounted to almost three hundred and thirty million dollars. He gave one million, five hundred thousand dollars to the Peace Palace at the Hague in the Netherlands. After the war began in Europe in 1914, he gave his home, Skibo Castle in Scotland, to the British Government for use as an army hospital.

卡内基的财富

卡内基一星期挣一美元二十美分

安德鲁·卡内基(1835—1919,美国工业家和慈善家)12岁就在一家纺织厂做线轴工,这个工作是把线缠到织机用的线轴上,他要从早六点干到晚六点。他每天挣20美分,就是一星期1.2美元。

安德鲁决定要找一份比线轴工好一些的工作。他努力地干活,几个月后他得到了一份新的工作——给提供织机蒸汽动力的炉子加煤,薪水是1.65美元。这个活又艰苦又危险,因为如果他不当心点的话,沸腾的容器就会爆炸并让他送命。但他的家里需要这笔高一点的薪水。

后来安德鲁还做过信使,每周2.5美元。对于一个14岁的孩子来说,这个工资可是很高了。他比一起的四个同事小,却跑得最快。不久他的薪水加到了3美元。如果哪天跑腿的事情少的话,他就会学习莫尔斯码,最终他有能力成为一名电报报务员,工资是每月25美元,他才16岁。

安德鲁·卡内基是美国历史上的最富有的人之一,可是当他越来越富有和年长后,他却对金钱开始反感。他说只要看到和碰到钱就会产生难受的感觉,也就分文不带。由于没钱买票，卡内基还被伦敦电车赶下来过。

他的公司估价五亿美元

1853 年，安德鲁·卡内基遇到了托马斯·斯科特，一位年轻的宾夕法尼亚铁路主管。铁路局方面根据卡内基的提议建立了自己电报线路。斯科特让安德鲁操作新电报并成为自己的办公助理。薪水是每月 35 美元，这为安德鲁在世界的崛起提供了绝好的机会。

1862 年他成立了拱顶石桥梁公司，以建设俄亥俄河上的第一座铁桥。1873 年他建立了托马森钢铁厂。

这个工厂自打开张就很成功。16 年的时间，美国的钢产量就超越了比自己炼钢早得多的英国。1888 年安德鲁·卡内基买入了和自己公司规模差不多的一家公司的控股权，还有匹兹堡附近的几家钢厂。他把这些企业合并成立了卡内基公司。这个公司包括矿山，钢厂，船舶和铁路，它把各地的原材料运进来，又把成品钢运出去。卡内基公司囊括了钢铁制造和派送的全部要素。1901 年他的公司以 5 亿美元的报价卖给了美国联合钢铁公司，它的发起人是美国著名的银行家约翰·皮埃彭特·摩根。之后摩根先生说卡内基是“世界上最富有的人”。他从一周 1.2 美元走到今天。

他怎样处理他的钱财呢？

卡内基用了 20 年的时间来散尽财富。他认为富人应该将他们不需要的那部分财富回归社会。他说富人如果不在有生之年把他的聚财能力用于为公益而散财的话，就会“难堪而死”。

他开始把钱用来建造免费的公共图书馆。1919 年，他已经建造了 3 000 座图书馆，总计价值 6 000 万美元以上。这些图书馆多数在美国，还有一些在加拿大、英国、新西兰，甚至远至斐济群岛。

卡内基的家乡，苏格兰的登菲尔慕林，收到了一份 400 万美元的礼物，这是为家乡的人们修建公园和运动场的。匹兹堡，这个他发财的地方，收到了一个音乐厅，一座博物馆，一个美术馆以及一个公共图书馆。

安德鲁·卡内基的公益投入几乎达到 3.3 亿美元。他给荷兰海牙和平宫提供了 150 万美元。1914 年战争在欧洲爆发后，他把自己家，位于苏格兰的斯基柏城堡给了英国政府，成为一座部队医院。

（孙尚奇　译）

The Truth about Walt Disney

He created Mickey Mouse and produced the first full-length animated movie. He invented the theme park and originated the modern multimedia corporation. For better or worse, his innovations have shaped our world and the way we experienced it.

The truth about Disney, who was described by an observant writer as "a tall, somber man who appeared to be under the lash of some private demon", is slightly less benign and a lot more interesting. Uncle Walt actually didn't have an avuncular bone in his body. Though he could manage a sort of gruff amiability with strangers, he was, in fact, a with drawn, suspicious and, above all, controlling nature. And with good—or anyway explicable —reason. For he was born to a poverty even more dire emotionally than it was economically. His father was one of those feckless figures who wandered seeking success in many occupations but always finding sour failure. He spared his children affection, but never the rod. They all fled him at the earliest possible moment.

Before leaving home at 16 to join the Red Cross Ambulance Corps during World War I, Walt, the youngest son, had discovered he could escape Dad's—and life' s— meanness in art classes. In the service he kept drawing, and when he was mustered out, he set up a shop as a commercial artist in Kansas City, Mo.. There he discovered animation, a new field, widely open to an ambitious young man determined to escape his father's sorry fate.

Reduced to living in his studio and eating cold beans out of a can, Disney endured the hard times any worthwhile success story demands. It was not until he moved to Los Angeles and partnered with his shrewd and kindly older brother Roy, who took care of business for him, that he began to prosper modestly. Even so, his first commercially viable creation, Oswald the Rabbit, was stolen from him. But, after that, Mickey made his appearance and became a symbol of the unconquerably chipper American spirit in the depths of Depression.

Predictably, he became the first Hollywood mogul to embrace television. The show with him as host for over a decade became not just a profit center for his company but also a promotional engine for all its works. In 1950s and 1960s, his compulsive attention was attracted by Disneyland.

Disneyland was another risk and Disney threw himself obsessively into the park's design, which anticipated many of the best features of modern urban planning, and into the "imagineering" by which the simulacrums of exotic, even dangerous creatures, places, fantasies could be unthreateningly reproduced. In his eyes, this park would be a small world, in which the dirt, rudeness, mischance and anything approaching authentic life would be totally eliminated. When Disneyland opened in 1955, Disney finally established a world of his own, which people had to experience on his terms.

真实的迪斯尼

他创造了米老鼠,制作了第一部标准长度的动画片,发明了主题公园和现代多媒体公司。不管好坏,他的发明极大地影响着世界和我们的体验方式。

一位观察家这样描写迪斯尼:"一位高大而神情忧郁的人,看上去像被某种不为人知的恶魔鞭打过。"真实的迪斯尼欠慈祥，但不乏有趣。沃尔特叔叔实际上没有慈爱，虽然面对陌生人他能装出和蔼的样子。事实上，他害羞而多疑，尤其是想控制一切。对此或许有些可以接受的理由。他出身于一个经济上贫困，感情上更加匮乏的家庭。他父亲是个不负责任的人，到处寻找发财的机会，但总是失败。他很少给孩子们父爱，但从不吝惜棍棒。孩子们也都尽早离开了他。

第一次世界大战期间，16 岁的沃尔特离开家参加了红十字救护队。在此之前，这个家中最小的孩子发现在艺术课上可以逃避父亲和生活的无趣。服役期间，他坚持绘画。退役后，他作为商业艺术家在密苏里的坎萨斯城开了一家商店。在那里他探索了动画制作，那是个新领域。这个雄心勃勃的年轻人决心逃脱父亲的悲惨命运。

迪斯尼住在摄影棚，吃着冰冷的罐头菜豆，度过了每个成功者都在所难免的艰难日子。后来他搬到洛杉矶与精明而又和蔼的兄长罗依合作。罗依帮他照看开始有些起色的生意。尽管如此，他的第一个有商业价值的创作奥斯瓦尔兔子还是被盗了。但是，那以后米老鼠出现了。在那时经济萧条的美国，米老鼠成了不可征服的活泼的美国精神的象征。

迪斯尼也是好莱坞第一个利用电视的大亨。十几年来他支持的电视节目不仅成为公司的赢利中心，而且大力推广了公司的作品。在 20 世纪 50 年代和 60 年代，他的注意力转向了迪斯尼乐园。

迪斯尼乐园是他的另一项冒险事业。迪斯尼全身心地投入到乐园的设计中，他融入了许多最优的现代城市规划以及奇异的幻想。甚至危险的生物、地方和想象都被他安全地复制出来。在迪斯尼的眼里，乐园就是个小世界。任何肮脏、粗鲁、不幸和接近真实生活的东西都被剔除掉。当1955年迪斯尼乐园开放时，迪斯尼终于建立了自己的世界。在那里，人们得按照他的理念行事。

Ray Kroc: Burger Master

McDonald's started an industry because a 52-year-old mixer salesman understood that we don't dine—we eat and run.

Kroc was adroit and perceptive in identifying popular trends. He sensed that America was a nation of people who ate out, as opposed to the Old World tradition of eating at home. Yet he also knew that people here wanted something different. Instead of structured, ritualistic restaurant with codes and routine, he gave them a simple, casual and identifiable restaurant with friendly service, low prices, no waiting and no reservations. The system eulogized the sandwich—no tableware to wash. One goes to McDonald's to eat, not to dine.

Kroc gave people what they wanted or, maybe, what he wanted. As he said, "The definition of salesmanship is the gentle art of letting the customer have it your way." He would remain the ultimate salesman, serving as a chairman of McDonald's Corp., the largest restaurant company in the world, from 1968 until his death in 1984.

In 1917, Ray Kroc was a brash 15-year-old who lied about his age to ioin the Red Cross as an ambulance driver. Sent to Connecticut for training, he never left for Europe because the war ended. So the teen had to find work, which he did, first as a piano player and then, in 1922, as a salesman for the Lily Tulip Cup Co..

Although he sold paper cups by day and played the piano for radio station at night, Kroc's ears were better tuned to the rhythms of commerce. In the course of selling paper cups he encountered Earl Prince, who had invented a five-spindle multimixer and was buying Lily cups by the truckload. Fascinated by the speed and efficiency of the machine, Kroc obtained exclusive marketing rights from Prince. Indefatigable, for the next 17 years he crisscrossed the country peddling the mixer.

On his travels he picked up the beat of a remarkable restaurant in San Bernardino, Calif., owned by two brothers, Dick and Mac McDonald, who had ordered eight mixers and had them churning away all day. Kroc saw the restaurant in

1954 and was entranced by the effectiveness of the operation. It was a hamburger restaurant, though not of the drive-in variety popular at the time. People had to get out of their cars to be served. The brothers had produced a very limited menu, concentrating on just a few items: hamburgers, cheeseburgers, french fries, soft drinks and milk shakes, all at the lowest possible prices.

Kroc, ever the instigator, started thinking about building McDonald's stores all over the U. S. —each of them equipped with eight multimixers whirring away, spinning off a steady stream of cash. The following day he pitched the idea of opening several restaurants to the brothers. They asked, "Who could we get to open them for us?" Kroc was ready: "Well, what about me?"

He was convinced that the best was ahead of him. He was even more convinced than the McDonalds and eventually cajoled them into selling out to him in 1961 for a paltry $2.7 million.

He was now free to run the business in his own way, but he never changed the fundamental format that had been devised by the brothers. Kroc added his own wrinkles, certainly. He was a demon for cleanliness. From the overall appearance, to the parking lot, to the kitchen floor, to uniforms, cleanliness was foremost and essential. "If you have time to lean, you have time to clean." was one of his favorite axioms. He was dead on, of course. The first impression you get from a restaurant, through the eyes and nose, is often what determines whether you'll go back.

By 1963 more than 1 billion hamburgers had been sold, a statistic that was displayed on a neon sign in front of each restaurant. That same year, the 500th McDonald opened and the famous clown, Ronald McDonald, made his debut. He soon became known to children throughout the country, and kids were critical in determining where the family ate. According to John Mariani in his remarkable book *America Eats Out*. "Within six years of airing his first national TV ad in 1965, the Ronald McDonald clown character was familiar to 96% of American children, far more than those who knew the name of the President of the United States."

Like many of America's great entrepreneurs, Kroc was not a creator— convenience food already existed in many forms, from Howard Johnson's to White Castle—but he had the cunning ability to grasp a concept with all its complexities and implement it in the best possible way. And that's as American as a cheeseburger.

雷·克罗克:汉堡大师

麦当劳之所以会开创一个行业,是因为一位52岁的食品搅拌器销售员明白了一个道理:人们已经不再正儿八经地“用膳”,而是吃完就走。

就发现流行趋势而言,克罗克可谓头脑灵活、感觉敏锐。他意识到美国是一个全民外出就餐的国度,这一点区别于欧洲人在家用餐的传统。但他同样知道,这里的人向往另类的用餐体验。麦当劳不是家一板一眼、架势十足的餐厅,也没有固定的礼仪和程式。克罗克为顾客们开设了一家简单、随意、易于识别的餐厅,这里有友善的服务、低廉的价格,顾客无需等待,也不用预定。麦当劳的整套机制对三明治推崇备至,因为它能省下清洁餐具的麻烦。人们去麦当劳是为了吃饭,不是用膳。

克罗克为人们提供了他们想要的,或者说,是他想要的东西。正如他说的那样:“推销的要旨,在于以温和的方式让消费者对你言听计从。”麦当劳后来成为全球最大的餐饮公司,克罗克也当上了公司的董事长,然而,从1968年开始,一直到他辞世的1984年,克罗克一直保持着推销员的本色。

1917年,雷·克罗克还是个15岁的莽撞少年。这一年,他通过谎报年龄加入了红十字会，并当上了一名救护车司机。他被送往康乃狄格州受训，却没能去往欧洲，因为还没等他奔赴前线，战争就已经结束了。于是，这位少年只得另谋职业，还真的找到了工作，他先是做了一名钢琴师，接着又在1922年当上了百合郁金香制杯公司的推销员。

就这样，他白天贩卖纸杯，夜间为广播电台弹奏钢琴，然而，他的耳朵却对商贸的律动更为敏感。他在销售纸杯时偶遇厄尔·普林斯，后者发明了一种带五根轴的多功能搅拌器，并一卡车一卡车地买进百合纸杯。克罗克被这种机械的速度和效率所吸引，于是从普林斯手里买下了它的专属营销权。在接下来的17年里，他不知疲倦地在国内穿梭往返、叫卖这种搅拌器。

他在旅途中发现了加州圣伯那地诺市一家出众的餐厅，餐厅的主人是迪克·麦当劳和麦克·麦当劳兄弟。弟兄俩订购了八套搅拌器，整天搅个不停。克罗克在1954年目睹了这家餐厅的经营，随即被其高效的运作方式迷住了。这是家出售汉堡的餐厅，却并非当时流行的免下车餐厅，顾客必须下车才会有人招呼。兄弟俩开发了一本内容非常有限的菜单，菜式只有几样：汉堡、奶酪汉堡、炸薯条、软饮料，外加奶昔，所有食物都以最低廉的价格出售。

克罗克开始设想在全美开设麦当劳的分店，每一家都要配备八台多轴搅拌器，它们得终日呼呼飞转，转出源源不断的现金。克罗克向来擅于鼓动别人,他第二天就竭力劝说兄弟俩另开几家店面。他们问他:“我们能找谁来帮忙开店呢?”克罗克对这个问题早有准备。“你们看我怎么样?”他答道。

他确定前途一片光明,甚至比麦当劳兄弟更有信心。1961 年,他终于哄得兄弟俩以区区 270 万美元的低价将公司拱手相让。

这下,克罗克可以按照自己的方式经营公司了,但他从未改动兄弟俩创立的基本格局。他理所当然地添加了自己的诀窍。他对清洁的追求可谓走火入魔,从餐厅的整体外观,到它的停车场,再到厨房的地板,乃至员工的制服,在这一切元素中,清洁乃是至关重要的。他最喜欢说的一句格言是:“有空倚靠,就不会没空清扫。”这话当然一点没错。顾客通过眼睛和鼻子对一家餐厅得出的第一印象,往往决定了他们是否会再度拜访。

到了 1963 年,麦当劳已经售出了超过 10 亿只汉堡,当时,每家分店门口的霓虹招牌上都打出了这个数字。同一年,麦当劳开出了第 500 家分店,著名的小丑罗纳德 · 麦当劳也首度登场,全国各地的孩子们很快就认识了他,而孩子对一家人在哪里用餐起着决定性作用。约翰 · 马利亚纳在他的杰作《美国外出就餐》中写道:“从 1965 年在全国播出第一个电视广告算起,小丑罗纳德 · 麦当劳在六年时间内就已为96%的美国儿童所熟知，这个比例远远超美国总统的名字在儿童中的知晓度。”

就像许多伟大的美国企业家一样，克罗克并非一名原创者——麦当劳风行之前，已经有了许多样式的方便食品，其中包括霍华德·约翰逊餐厅和“白色城堡”汉堡店——但克罗克却有种特殊的狡黠，他能把握错综复杂的概念，并使其发挥最佳功用。这一点十分美国化，就像奶酪汉堡那样。

（高天羽 译）

Bill Gates: Who Saw Computers as a Way of Making Money

One big difference between Gates and other early software entrepreneurs is that, whereas the others were bright kids from middle-class homes who achieved success beyond their expectations, Gates was born to rule.

Gates attended Lakeside School, one of the best private schools in the Seattle area, and there he met Paul Allen, who was three years older. The two began spending a lot of time in the school's computer room. In 1971, when Gates was sixteen, he wrote a program that made it easier for cities to collect traffic statistics. That same year, he and Allen started a company called Traf-o-Data. In the Lakeside yearbook for 1973, Gates' senior year, there is a picture of Gates in the computer room with a stocking cap pulled over his head and lying on a table, over the caption "Who is this man?"

Gates and Allen sometimes talked about how cool it would

be to design the software for the first personal computer, which appeared to be on the horizon, but this was not a serious career goal of Bill's. His father wanted him to become a lawyer. "When I was in college, it was really hard to pick a career, because everything seemed so attractive, and when you had to pick a specific one you had to say no to all the others," Gates said. "I'd think, well, if I went to that law firm some partner might not like me, and they might assign me to these crummy cases, and I'd think, Well, God, that could be really crummy." The question was settled in dramatic fashion in December, 1974, when Allen, who was working in Boston, passed a newsstand in Harvard Square and saw on the cover of *Popular Electronics* a computer called the Altair 8800. The Altair 8800 was the first computer that ordinary electronics hobbyists could afford to buy and that people with reasonable technical knowledge could assemble in their homes. Basically, it was the first personal computer. Allen bought the magazine, rushed over to Gates' dorm, and showed it to him. "Look!" Allen said. "It's going to happen! I told you this was going to happen! And we're going to miss it!"

They called Ed Roberts, the man who created the Altair, and told him that they had written a version of programming language called BASIC for his computer. That wasn't true. It was an early use of a now common strategy in the computer industry, and at Microsoft in particular: announcing products that don't exist (known in the industry as "vaporware") in order to discourage possible competitors. After talking to Roberts, Bill and Paul went on an eight-week code-writing binge, with Gates writing most of the code, often falling asleep at the keyboard, dreaming in code, waking up, and immediately starting to write code again, with no real transition between dreaming and waking—just code. ("It was the coolest program I ever wrote," Gates later said.) At the end of the eighth week, Allen flew out to Albuquerque, met with Roberts, loaded the software into the Altair, and typed "PINTER 2 + 2." The Altair spat out "4". The program worked.

By the end of 1975, Gates and Allen had founded a company, Microsoft, to sell their BASIC. Now came what is perhaps the pivotal moment in the early history of the software industry. Computer hobbyists who had bought the Altair was dismayed to find that it didn't come with the software to operate it, and were even more dismayed when they learned that they had to buy the software for four hundred and fifty dollars from Microsoft. At that time, no one thought of software as something you paid for. Software was just rolls of paper tape with little holes punched in it. A hacker would write a cool piece of software for fun, copy it, and give it away to his friends. Altair owners began to do the same thing with Micro-soft's BASIC. Then, in February of 1976, Gates published "An Open Letter to Hobbyists" in the Altair newsletter, and the letter now stands as a sort of "Magna Carta" of the software industry—the underpinning of the intellectual-property structure. It stated, "As the majority of hobbyists must be aware, most of you steal your software," and went on to argue that software was just as much a commodity as hardware, because it represented someone's intellectual work, and that the creators of the software should be compensated just as creators of hardware were.

Software is sometimes said to be to the age of information as oil was to the age of the machine. Software is what makes information systems operate. Software is like a natural resource, except that its source is not in the earth but in the human mind: people carry tools of software in their heads. Its lack of physical existence makes its importance easy to underestimate. I. B. M., which was one of the great business organizations in history, and which was perfectly placed to own the personal computer business, disastrously failed to appreciate the importance of the software Gates designed for it. Because I. B. M. thought the money was going to be in the hardware, in the computers themselves, it allowed Gates to retain the rights to MS-DOS. During the nineteen-eighties, the PC was cloned by other American manufacturers and by the Japanese, who could make and sell the machines more cheaply than I. B. M. could, but no one knew how to clone MS-DOS, and Bill Gates collected a fee for every PC and every PC clone sold in the world.

Gates was different from most hackers in one important aspect: Hackers were interested in computers as a hobby, mostly just for fun, whereas Gates always saw computers as a way of making money.

比尔·盖茨：把计算机看作挣钱门道的人

盖茨与其他的早期软件企业家的最大不同在于，这些人出生于中产阶级家庭，他们所取得的成就已经让家人欣喜不已。而盖茨生就是王者。

盖茨在西雅图最好的私立湖滨学校就读,就是在那里他遇见了长他三岁的保罗·艾伦。这两人经常泡在学校的计算机房里。1971年,16岁的他写出了一个帮助简化城市交通数据处理的程序,同年他和艾伦创办了"交通数据公司"。湖滨学校1973年的年鉴上还有一张高年级的盖茨戴着绒线帽横在计算机房桌子上的照片,标题是:"他是谁?"

盖茨和艾伦曾经憧憬过为第一台个人计算机写软件的美梦,这件事当时似乎并非完全不靠谱,可这不能成为盖茨的职业。他父亲希望他成为律师,"当我在大学时,未来充满诱惑,让你无法抉择,最终你不得不选择一个,而对其他的说不了。"盖茨说道,"我想如果我去了律师事务所,那里的有些人未必喜欢我,他们让我去处理些倒霉的案子,我想,好吧,上帝啊,这才是我真正的倒霉。"到了1974年12月,事情发生了戏剧性的变化,当在波士顿工作的艾伦路过哈佛广场的一个书报亭时,看见《大众电子》杂志封面的一台计算机叫作Altair 8800,这台机器是第一台普通电子爱好者买得起的计算机,并且需要这些人回家自己利用技术组装出来,我们基本可以称呼它为第一批家用计算机。艾伦买了杂志,冲到盖茨的宿舍,对他说:"看啊,即将开始了,我对你说过会开始的,我们差点就错过了。"

他们给Altair的制造者Ed罗伯特打电话,告诉他自己已经为这台计算机写好了一个程序语言版本,叫 BASIC。实际上当时这个程序语言还没有出炉呢。现在的计算机行业,特别是微软,常常使用这种战略——发布还不存在的产品(术语叫雾件)以打击潜在的竞争者。在和罗伯特通话后,比尔和艾伦用了八周的时间疯狂地扑在程序写作上,盖茨更是常常趴在键盘上睡着,做梦,又醒过来,立刻投入编程,似乎梦中与现实只有编码一个中心,他完成了编程工作的大半("这是我编写过的最棒的程序。"盖茨后来这样说过。)。到了第八周周末,艾伦飞去罗伯特那里将程序装入 Altair,然后输入"测试 2 +2",计算机马上跳出"4",程序成功了。

到了 1975 年末,盖茨和艾伦组建了微软公司,出售 BASIC。现在可以这样说,这个时刻成为软件行业历史上的关键时点。买了 Altair 的那些计算机爱好者们会痛苦地发现没有软件运行这台机器,而更沮丧的是他们必须花 450 美元从微软购买运行软件。在那个时代没人觉得软件是需要付钱的东西,软件似乎只是一卷上面带有小孔的纸。那时的程序员就是为了好玩而编一段小程序,并且复制,送给亲朋好友。而现在 Altair 的拥有者们也可以用微软的 BASIC 当一回程序员了。到了 1976 的 2 月,盖茨在 Altair 通讯上发表了"致爱好者的公开信",这封信现在已经被认为是软件行业的"宪法"——它构建了知识产权的框架。它说道:"多数的电脑爱好者必须知道,你们中大多数人使用的软件是偷来的。"

另外它还认为软件和邮件一样也是商品，因为它含有人的智力付出，因此软件的设计者和硬件的生产者一样，也需要得到补偿。

人们有时把信息时代的软件比喻为工业时代的石油。正是由于软件才能使信息系统得以运转。就此而言，软件就像自然资源，不同的是它存在于人的大脑，人用大脑产生软件，而不是像石油一样存在于地下。由于它缺乏物理性状而常常被人低估价值。历史上最大的商业公司之一，在个人计算机领域有着出色表现的 IBM，就对盖茨为其设计的软件重要性缺乏正确的认识而失去良机。IBM 认为计算机的硬件本身才是赚钱的正路，所以它让盖茨保留了 MS-DOS 的产权。到了 20 世纪 80 年代，个人计算机技术开始为其他厂家所掌握，其中有美国本土的也有日本企业，他们的机器比 IBM 便宜，但没有一个厂家能够生产出和 DOS 一样的软件，而盖茨则从世界各地的每台计算机和计算机厂家那里收取到费用。

盖茨和多数电脑爱好者的一个重大的区别在于，他们将计算机作为一个爱好，大多数就是为了开心，而盖茨始终把计算机看作是赚钱的工具。

（孙尚奇　译）

MR. "Sony": Akio Morita's Extraordinary Drive

In 1993, Akio Morita—Mr. Sony—fell to the ground during a game of tennis. The co-founder and chairman of the board had suffered a stroke. He has since been in a wheelchair. This is particularly sad, as Morita had never been able to sit still and relax. At 72, he was playing tennis at 7 a. m. each Tuesday. He never seemed to be tired when he was playing tennis. Many people would play with their instructors, and if they felt tired, they would just have a break. Not him. He challenged everybody, including young athletes.

This was in keeping with a man who created one of the first global corporations. He saw long before his contemporaries that a shrinking world could present enormous opportunities for a company that could think beyond its own borders, both physically and psychologically. And he pursued that strategy with his relentless brand of energy in every market, particularly in the U. S.. It is notable that in 1998, according to a Harries survey, Sony is rated the No. 1 brand name by American consumers, ahead of Coca-Cola and General Electric.

The best way to describe Morita's extraordinary drive is to scan his schedule for the two-month period immediately preceding his stroke. He took trips from his home base in Tokyo to New Jersey, Washington, Chicago, San Francisco, Los Angeles, San Antonio, Dallas, Britain, Barcelona and Paris. During that time he met with Queen Elizabeth II, General Electric chief Jack Welch, future French President Jacques Chirac, Isaac Stern and many other politicians, bureaucrats and business associates. He attended two concerts and a movie; took four trips within Japan; appeared at eight receptions; played nine rounds of golf; was guest of honor at a wedding ceremony; and went to work as usual for 17 days at Sony headquarters. Morita's schedule had been decided on more than a year in advance. Whenever there was a small opening, Morita would immediately and strategically fill it by arranging a meeting with someone he wanted to become acquainted with or catch up with. Unlike so many executives who remove themselves from the rest of the corporate pyramid, he was always in the middle of the actions.

Morita was a workaholic, but he was also a playaholic. He followed art and music, and was a sports fanatic. In his 60s he took up wind surfing and scuba diving and started skiing to ensure good exercise through the winter. He loved to water-ski and even crafted a water-resistant microphone on a handle, connected by a wire on the ski rope to a speaker on the boat so he could relay instructions to his wife Yoshiko. He was so proud of this invention. To simply have a good time, he would invent and perfect such a product.

The Walkman is just such an invention. Morita watched as his children and their friends play music from morning until night. He noticed people listening to music in their cars and carrying large stereos to the beach and the park. Sony's engineering department was generally opposed to the concept of a tape player without a recording function (it would be added later), but Morita would not be denied. He insisted on a product that sounded like a high-quality car stereo yet was portable and allowed the user to listen while doing something else—thus the name Walkman.

The creation of the name Sony highlights Morita's intuition and determination to communicate globally. He wanted a name recognizable everywhere: creative, Roman letters, short and catchy. Morita and Ibuka pored over dictionaries and found the word sonus, which in Latin means "sound". In addition, the word sonny was part of the pop vernacular in America at the time, and they thought it suggested a company made up of young people with abundant energy. The combination of the two formed Sony.

Morita achieved more than most could imagine in one lifetime. If he had been able to read the paper reporting Sony as the No. 1 consumer brand in the U. S., he would have smiled from his beachside mansion in Oahu and said, "Of course! I told you so! After all, Sony was made in the U. S. A.!"

"索尼"先生：盛田昭夫的超凡魄力

1993 年，"索尼先生"盛田昭夫在一场网球赛中倒地不起。这位索尼公司的创始人兼董事会主席遭遇了一次中风。从那以后，他的日子就一直在轮椅上度过。这对盛田来说尤其悲惨，因为他此前从来没有机会静坐放松。时年 72 岁的他每周四早上七点都去打网球。他在玩网球的时候从来不显得劳累。别人大多是和教练一齐打球,觉得累了就休息一阵。他不是。他向每个人发起挑战,包括年轻的运动员。

这份斗志倒是配得上这样一位第一批全球企业的创办者。早在他的同龄人之前,他就明白了一个道理:对一家在物质和精神上的思考都能超越自身界限的公司而言,一个日益缩小的世界将会提供巨大的机会。他还以招牌式的进取精神,在每一个市场实施自己的全球战略,尤以美国为重点。值得一提的是,根据一项1988年的哈里斯调查,当时的索尼已跃升美国消费者提名的第一品牌,领先于可口可乐和通用电器。

要描述盛田的非凡干劲,最好的办法就是看一看他中风之前两个月内的行程。他从位于东京的公司总部出发,依次造访了新泽西、华盛顿、芝加哥、旧金山、洛杉矶、圣安东尼奥、达拉斯、英国、巴塞罗那和巴黎。在这段时间里,他会见了英国女王伊丽莎白二世、通用电器总裁杰克·韦尔奇、后来成为法国总统的雅克·希拉克、艾萨克·斯特恩以及许多政客、官僚和商业伙伴。此外,他还听了两场音乐会,看了一场电影,在日本境内旅行了四次,参加了八场宴会,打了九局高尔夫球,作为嘉宾出席了一场婚礼,剩下的十七天都照常去索尼总部上班。盛田的时间表早在一年之前就已排定,中间一旦出现空缺,他就会立刻巧妙地安插一次会面,对方通常是一个他想要结识或赶超的人。许多总裁都会脱离公司的底层运营，而盛田却总是亲自参与到公司的各项行动中去。

盛田工作成瘾，但同样耽于玩乐。他追逐艺术和音乐，同时热衷运动。他在60多岁开始玩风帆冲浪和潜水，为了确保能在冬季得到足够运动，他还滑起了雪。他热爱滑水，甚至在一块手柄上精心制作了一只防水麦克风，麦克风通过绳索上的电线同前方船上的喇叭相连，盛田以此向船上的妻子山口下达指令。他对自己的这项发明十分自豪。他会单单为了寻开心而发明类似的产品，并加以改进。

随身听就是这样一件发明。盛田看见自己的孩子和他们的朋友一天到晚播放音乐，还注意到人们在自己的车里听音乐，并带着大型立体声装置去海滩、上公园。他由此萌发了随身听的想法。索尼的工程部却一致反对开发不带录音功能的磁带播放装置（录音功能是后来添加的），但盛田不会任凭自己的提议遭人否决。他坚持开发这样一种产品：它必须能在音效上比肩高音质汽车音响，但又能随身携带、能让使用者边听音乐边干其他事——“随身听”的名字就是这么来的。

“Sony”这个名称昭示了盛田的灵感和通告全球的决心。他想要一个尽人皆识的名字，它必须有创意、由罗马字母组成、短小又便于记忆。盛田和深井钻研了几本字典，发现了“sonus”这个字，它在拉丁语中的意思是“声响”。此外，当时在美国还有句流行的口头禅叫"sonny"("小弟"),两人认为,这句口语能让人觉得公司是由活力充沛的年轻人组成的。于是,"sonus"和"sonny"就结合产生了"Sony"。

盛田在一生中取得的成就超过了大多数人的想象。如果他能在报纸上读到索尼成为美国消费者心目中的第一品牌,那他一定会在瓦胡岛的海滨别墅微笑着说:"那是当然!我跟你说过!索尼毕竟是在美国发迹的!"

(高天羽　译)

V 运动员

Athletes

Pelé: Football Phenomenon

Performance at a high level in any sport is to exceed the ordinary human scale. But Pelé's performance transcended that of the ordinary star by as much as the star exceeds ordinary performance. He scored an average of a goal in every international game he played—the equivalent of a baseball player's hitting a home run in every World Series game over 15 years. Between 1956 and 1974, Pelé scored a total of 1, 220 goals—not unlike hitting an average of 70 home runs every year for a decade and a half.

While he played, Brazil won the World Cup, staged quadrennially, three times in 12 years. He scored five goals in a game six times, four goals 30 times and three goals 90 times. And he did so not aloofly or disdainfully—as do many modern stars—but with an infectious joy that caused even the teams over which he triumphed to share in his pleasure, for it is no disgrace to be defeated by a phenomenon defying emulation.

He was born across the mountains from the great coastal cities of Brazil, in the impoverished town of Tres Coracoes. Nicknamed Dico by his family, he was called Pelé by soccer friends, a word whose origins escape him. Dico shined shoes until he was discovered at the age of 11 by one of the country's premier players, Waldemar de Brito. Four years later, De Brito brought Pelé to Sao Paulo and declared to the disbelieving directors of the professional team in Santos, "This boy will be the greatest soccer player in the world." He was quickly legend. By the next season, he was the top scorer in his league. As the "Times of London" would later say, "How do you spell Pelé? G-O-D." He has been known to stop war: both sides in Nigeria's civil war called a 48-hour cease-fire in 1967 so Pelé could play an exhibition match in the capital of Lagos.

To understand Pelé's role in soccer, some discussion of the nature of the game is necessary. No team sport evokes the same sort of primal, universal passion as soccer. During the World Cup, the matches of the national football teams impose television schedules on the rhythm of life. Last year I attended a dinner for leading members of the British establishment and distinguished guests from all over the world at the staid Spencer House in London. The hosts had the bad luck to have chosen the night of the match between England and Argentina—always a blood feud, compounded on this occasion by the memory of the Falklands crisis. The impeccable audience (or at least enough of it to influence the hosts) insisted that television sets be set up at strategic locations, during both the reception and the dinner. The match went into overtime and required a penalty shoot-out afterward, so the main speaker did not get to deliver his message until 11 p. m. And since England lost, the audience was not precisely in a mood for anything but mourning.

When France finally won the World Cup, Paris was paralyzed with joy for nearly 48 hours, Brazil by dejection for a similar period of time. I was in Brazil in 1962 when the national team won the World Cup in Chile. Everything stopped for two days while Rio celebrated a premature carnival.

Pelé is a different phenomenon from the baseball or football star. Soccer stars are dependent on their teams even while transcending them. To achieve mythic status as a soccer player is especially difficult because the peak performance is generally quite short—only the fewest players perform at the top of their game for more than five years. Incredibly, Pelé performed at the highest level for 18 years, scoring 52 goals in

1973, his 17th year. Contemporary soccer superstars never reach even 50 goals a season. For Pelé, who had thrice scored more than 100 goals a year, it signaled retirement.

The mythic status of Pelé derives as well from the way he incarnated the character of Brazil's national team. Its style affirms that virtue without joy is a contradiction in terms. Its players are the most acrobatic, if not always the most proficient. Brazilian teams play with a contagious exuberance. When those yellow shirts go on the attack—which is most of the time—and their fans cheer to the intoxicating beat of samba bands, soccer becomes a ritual of fluidity and grace. In Pelé's day, the Brazilians epitomized soccer as fantasy.

I saw Pelé at his peak only once, at the final of the World Cup in 1970. Brazil's opponent was Italy, which played its tough defense coupled with sudden thrusts to tie the game 1–1, demoralizing the Brazilians. Italy could very easily have massed its defense even more, until its frantic opponent began making the mistakes that would encompass its ruin. But, led by Pelé, Brazil paid no attention. Attacking as if the Italians were a practice team, the Brazilians ran them into the ground, 4–1.

I saw Pelé a few times afterward, when he was playing

for the New York Cosmos. He was no longer as fast, but he was as exuberant as ever. By then, Pelé had become an institution. Most modern fans never saw him play, yet they somehow feel he is part of their lives. He made the transition from superstar to mythic figure.

贝利：足球奇迹

任何高水平运动员的运动技能肯定超越一般人，而贝利的才能比这些明星还要高得多。他在 1956 年到 1974 年间参加的国际大赛中，共计射入 1 220 个球，如果算一下年度平均数的话，相当于一个棒球手要连续 15 年在每年大赛中击出 70 个本垒打。

他帮助巴西队在连续 12 年的四届世界杯中赢得三次冠军。他有六次在一场比赛中进 5 球，三十次在一场比赛中进 4 球，九十次进 3 球。他不像现在的某些球星常常被人诟病，他所取得的成就甚至连他的对手球队也心悦诚服，共同欢庆，因为被天才击败并非奇耻大辱。

他出生于巴西沿海大城市附近山区里的一个贫穷小镇——特雷斯·科拉索斯镇。家里人叫他迪可，而足球圈内朋友则称呼他为贝利，这个名字从此伴随他一生。迪可直到

11 岁时才被原国家队的主力球员之一的瓦尔德马·德·布利托相中,4 年后德·布利托将贝利带到圣保罗并对桑托斯球队的经理们说:"这个孩子将会成为世界上最伟大的足球运动员。"虽然他们当时并不相信,可贝利的传奇很快开始了,在第二个赛季,他已经成为联赛中的顶级球员。如同《伦敦时报》后来所说:"你应该怎么拼写贝利? G-O-D(上帝)。"他还曾经停止过战争:1967 年贝利来到内战中的尼日利亚,交战双方达成协议,停火 48 小时,以便贝利能够在首都拉各斯进行一场表演赛。

要解读贝利的作用,就有必要对足球的一些基本情况进行了解。没有一项团队运动能够像足球一样引起全球的热情,在世界杯期间,国家队间的比赛充满了日常电视节目。去年,我出席了一个在斯宾塞宫举行的英伦本地企业领导招待晚宴,其中还有许多来自世界各地的尊贵来宾。主办者显然错误地选择了晚宴的时刻——那天晚上有一场英格兰与阿根廷的足球赛,这两个国家队之间本来就是旧账未断,后来又因为福克兰群岛危机而平添新伤。这些尊贵的宾客(至少对主办者而言,确实重要)坚持在整个招待会期间要把电视机放在显著的位置。球赛进入加时,最终进行点球决胜,因此直到午夜 11 点,主要的致辞都未能进行,由于英格兰输了球,来宾的注意力已经不在晚宴上,悲痛的气氛弥漫全场。

当法国最终赢得世界杯之时,巴黎几乎欢腾了将近 48

小时,而同时,失败的巴西全国则陷入了沮丧的氛围中。1962 年巴西队夺得智利世界杯冠军时,我恰好在巴西,里约全城进行了狂欢节般地庆祝,其他所有的事务的钟摆都似乎停止了两天。

贝利的才华与棒球和橄榄球的球星都不同。足球明星,即使是超级巨星也离不开球队团队的支持。作为一个足球运动员,要想将自己的巅峰状态维持 5 年以上而达到名垂青史的地位非常难。令人难以置信的是,贝利将巅峰状态维持了 18 年,即使是在他职业生涯的第 17 个年头,也就是 1973 年,他依然有 52 个进球,当代的超级巨星们也未必能在一个赛季里进球 50 个。对贝利这位三次一年内进球过百的人来说,这种数据意味着要退休了。

贝利神话般的成绩也得益于他为之献身的巴西国家队的风格。这支球队将“快乐与技术”融为一体,即使他们未必总是技高一筹,但他们总是充满激情,球员踢球如杂耍般轻松。当这支黄色军团进攻时(他们大部分时间都在进攻),他们的球迷便会随桑巴节奏而如痴如醉,足球赛成了流动而优美的宗教仪式。在贝利时代,巴西人迷醉于足球之中。

贝利巅峰时期的比赛,我只看过一次。在 1970 年的世界杯决赛中,巴西与意大利争夺冠军,后者用坚固的防守和突然的反击使得比分一度维持在一比一。意大利人似乎对防守得心应手,他们往往会使对手心浮气躁而导致失误并最终走向毁灭。但贝利带领的巴西队对此毫不在意，他们如同打练习赛般轻松地将比分定格在四比一上。

此后，我还看过几次他的比赛，当他加盟纽约宇宙队时，他已不再速度超群，但激情依旧。后来他成为一个神话。现代的大多数球迷都没见过他的表演，可是还是将他视为生活的一部分。贝利，完成了一个巨星转变为圣人的历程。

（孙尚奇　译）

Muhammad Ali: The World's Most Adored Athlete

Oliver Wendell Holmes once observed that every profession is great that is greatly pursued. Boxing in the early '60s, largely controlled by the Mob, was in a moribund state until Muhammad Ali—Cassius Clay, in those days—appeared on the scene. "Just when the sweet science appears to lie like a painted ship upon a painted ocean," wrote A. J. Liebling, "a new hero. . . comes along like a Moran tug to pull it out of the ocean."

Though Ali won the gold medal at the Rome Olympics in 1960, at the time the experts didn't think much of his boxing skills. His head, eyes wide, seemed to float above the action. Rather than slip a punch, the traditional defensive move, it was his habit to sway back, bending at the waist— a tactic that appalled the experts. Lunacy.

Nor did they approve of his personal behavior: the self-promotions, his affiliation with the Muslims and giving up his "slave name" for Muhammad Ali, the poetry or the quips. At the press conferences, the reporters were sullen. Ali would turn on them. "Why ain't you taking notice?" or "Why ain't you laughing?"

The public as well had a hard time accepting him. Then, three years after Ali defended the championship, there came the public vilification for his refusal to join the army during the Vietnam War —"I ain't got no quarrel with them Viet Cong"— one of the more telling remarks of the era. The government prosecuted him for draft dodging, and the boxing commissions took away his license. He was idle for 3.5 years at the peak of his career. In 1971 the Supreme Court ruled that the government had acted improperly. But Ali bore the commissions no ill will.

There were no lawsuits to get his title back through the courts. No need, he said, to punish them for doing what they thought was right. Quite properly, in his mind, he won back the title in the ring, knocking out George Foreman in the eighth round of their fight in Zaire —"The Rumble in the Jungle."

Ali was asked on a television show what he would have done with his life, given a choice. After an awkward pause—a rare thing, indeed—he admitted he couldn't think of anything other than boxing. That is all he had ever wanted or wished for. He couldn't imagine anything else. He defended boxing as a sport: "You don't have to be hit in boxing. People don't understand that."

He was wrong. Joe Frazier, speaking of their fight, said he had hit Ali with punches that would have brought down a building. Coaxed into fights by his managers long after he should have retired, and perhaps because he loved the sport too much to leave it, Ali ended up being punished by the likes of Leon Spinks and Larry Holmes, who took little pleasure in what they were doing.

Oscar Wilde once suggested that you kill the thing you love. In Ali's case, it was the reverse: what he loved, in a sense, killed him. The man who was the most loquacious of athletes now says almost nothing: he moves slowly through the crowds and signs autographs. He has probably signed more autographs than any other athletes ever, living or dead. It is his principal activity at home, working at his desk. He was once denied an autograph by his idol, Sugar Ray Robinson, and vowed he would never turn anyone down. The volume of mail is enormous.

The ceremonial leave-taking of great athletes can impart indelible memories, even if one remembers them from the scratchy newsreels of time—Babe Ruth with the doffed cap at home plate, Lou Gehrig's voice echoing in the vast hollows of Yankee Stadium. Muhammad Ali's was not exactly a leave-taking, but it may have seemed so to the estimated 3 billion or so television viewers who saw him open the Atlanta Olympics in 1996. Outfitted in a white gym suit that eerily made him seem to glisten against a dark night sky, he approached the unlit saucer with his flaming torch, his free arm trembling visibly from the effects of Parkinson's.

It was a kind of epiphany that those who watched realized how much they missed him and how much he had contributed to the world of sport. Students of boxing will pore over the trio of Ali-Frazier fights, which rank among the greatest in fistic history, as one might read three acts of a great drama. They would remember the shenanigans, the Ali Shuffle, the Rope-a-Dope, the fact that Ali had brought beauty and grace to the most uncompromising of sports. And they would marvel that through the wonderful excesses of skill and character, he had become the most famous athlete, indeed, the best-known personage in the world.

穆罕默德·阿里：世界最仰慕的运动员

奥利弗·温德尔·霍姆斯曾经在调查后说，每个职业都有其出彩的地方，它们也为许多人所追捧。可在60年代早期，拳击还基本受控于黑帮之下，并且很不景气。这种情形直到穆罕默德·阿里——原名卡修斯·克雷——的出现才得以改变。里博灵写道："当拳击的技巧如同一艘画出来的船在画出来的海洋上停滞之时，一个新的英雄出现了，就像神话英雄般地把它拖离原地。"

虽然阿里在1960年的罗马奥运会上赢得了金牌，但当时专家们还是不看好他的拳击技巧，他的头部、眼睛通常都会暴露在外。而不是像传统的移动防守那样躲闪打击。他通常都是弯曲着腰部向后摇摆，专家们都对这种战术感到惊讶，甚至认为有些愚蠢。

他们也不太赞同他的个人行为方式——自夸，对穆斯林的认同归属感，为了穆罕默德·阿里的名字而舍弃自己的"奴隶姓名"以及他作的诗和那些讽刺的言语。在记者招待会上如果记者们不太兴奋，阿里就会掉转方向对他们说"为何你们不记录?"或是"为何你们不笑?"

公众也有段时间不能接受他。在他卫冕冠军的三年后，发生了公众对他拒绝参军去越南的强烈指责——“我与越南大兵无冤无仇”——成为那个时代最流行的语言。政府以逃避兵役罪指控他，拳击委员会吊销他的执照，他在自己的职业巅峰期时，却不得不闲赋在家三年半。到了1971年最高法院裁定政府行为失当，但阿里认为委员会并无恶意。

当时也没有法律条文可以让他的头衔通过法院重归于他。他说，没必要因为做了他们自己认为是正确的事情而惩罚他们。有了这份心中的平静，他在扎伊尔的那场号称“丛林大战”比赛中，第八回合击倒乔治·福尔曼，终于在拳击场上赢回了冠军。

在一次电视节目里，他被问道，如果再有选择的话，他会选择做什么。经过一会少有的沉思后，他依然认为是拳击。这就是他所想和所愿的，其他事情都无法替代。他认为拳击就是一项体育运动：“你不是只在比赛中被击中，人们不了解这项运动的本质。”

可是他错了。乔·弗雷泽在谈及他们之间的较量时说，他打击阿里的拳头足以撼动一幢大楼。由于深爱着这项运动而难以割舍，他在本应该退休时禁不住经纪人的诱惑而再次出战。阿里最终受到了利昂·斯宾克斯和拉里·霍尔姆斯这些人的痛击，而这些人很少像他那么热爱拳击。

奥斯卡·王尔德曾经说人们会毁坏所爱的东西。阿里的一生中却是相反,某种意义上应该是被所爱的东西而害。这位曾经最健谈的运动员现在几乎不说话:他缓慢地穿过围拥着要求签名的人群,他可能是世界历史上为人签名最多的运动员,他现在的主要活动就是在家里的办公桌前为他人签名。他曾经遭到他的偶像休格雷·罗宾逊的拒绝签名,所以他发誓他不会拒绝任何人,来要求签名的信笺不计其数。

伟大的运动员的告别仪式总是令人难忘,虽然有时人们只是从那些已经模糊的新闻纪录片里可以唤起记忆——鲍比·鲁斯在本垒板上受到全场的脱帽礼、罗·葛雷克的嗓音在扬基队棒球场回荡。穆罕默德·阿里没有这样的仪式,可是他在 1996 年亚特兰大奥运会上点燃了开幕的火炬,对于观看了开幕式的 30 亿观众来说,这在某种意义上就是告别仪式了。他身着白色的运动装,衬托在黑色的夜空里更加醒目,他拿着火炬走向火炬台,那只空着的手不停地抖动,让人明显看出他受到的帕金森综合征影响。

这个瞬间让所有观看开幕式的人感到人们对他的了解太少,而他却对体育贡献了太多。学拳击的都会仔细地观看阿里与弗雷泽之间的三次大战,因为它们是拳击运动中最伟大的比赛之一,而你就如同能一气呵成地读完一个伟大的剧作的三幕。他们会记住,虚晃,阿里蝴蝶步,倚绳战术,以及阿里为最坚强的体育运动带来的优雅和美丽。他们会由于他的极其鲜明的技术和性格而赞叹不已。他是世界上最有名的运动员,更准确地说是世界上最知名的人。

（孙尚奇　译）

Michael Jordan: The God in Youth

There were already signs that Jordan had a good deal of talent. Harvest Smith, a classmate and close friend who in those days played basketball with him practically very day, thought he was the best player on their ninth-grade team—he was small, but he was every quick.

The summer after ninth grade, Jordan and Smith both went to Pop Herring's basketball camp. Neither of them had yet come into his body, and almost all of the varsity players, two and sometimes three years older, seemed infinitely stronger at that moment when a year or two in physical development can make all the difference. In Smith's mind there was no doubt which of the two of them was the better player—it was Michael by far. But on the day the varsity cuts were announced. Smith's name was on it, Michael's was not.

It was the worst day of Jordan's young life. The list was alphabetical, so he focused on where the Js should be, and it wasn't there, and he kept reading and rereading the list, hoping somehow that he had missed it, or that the alphabetical listing had been done incorrectly. That day he went home by himself and went to his room and cried. Smith understood what was happening—Michael, he knew, never wanted you to see him when he was hurt.

"We knew Michael was good," Fred Lynch, the Laney assistant coach, said later, "but we wanted him to play more and we thought the jayvee was better for him." He easily became the best player on the jayvee that year. He simply dominated the play, and he did it not by size but with quickness. There were games in which he would score forty points. He was so good, in fact, that the jayvee games became quite popular. The entire varsity began to come early so they could watch him play in the jayvee games.

Smith noticed that while Jordan had been wildly competitive before he had been cut, after the cut he seemed even more competitive than ever, as if determined that it would never happen again. His coaches noticed it, too. "The first time I ever saw him, I had no idea who Michael Jordan was. I was helping to coach the Laney varsity," said Ron Coley. "We went over to Goldsboro, which was our big rival, and I entered the gym when the jayvee game was just ending up. There were nine players on the court just coasting, but there was one kid playing his heart out. The way he was playing I thought his team was down one point with two minutes to play. So I looked up at the clock and his team was down twenty points and there was only one minute to play. It was Michael, and I quickly learned he was always like that."

He was as driven as ever, the hardest-working player on the team in practice. If he thought that his teammates were not working hard enough, he would get on them himself, and on occasion he pushed the coaches to get on them. Suddenly Laney High had the beginning of a very good basketball team, and its rising star was Michael Jordan.

迈克尔·乔丹：青年的偶像

迈克尔的天赋早已有所显露。维斯特·史密斯是他的同班同学和亲密伙伴，当时基本上每天都和他一起打篮球。他觉得乔丹是九年级球队中最出色的。他身材不高但非常灵活。

读完九年级的那个夏天，乔丹和史密斯一同参加了波普·赫里的篮球夏令营。他俩那时还未长大成人,而几乎所有其他队员都比他们大两三岁。当时,大一两岁在体魄上就大相径庭,因而看上去都比他们强壮得多。在史密斯眼里,他们两人谁更出色是毫无疑问的——迈克尔比他强多了。但是当宣布校队队员筛选名单时,有史密斯的名字,却没有迈克尔。

对于年轻的乔丹来说,那是最糟糕的一天。名单是按字母顺序排列的,他就注意看"J"字所在的地方,可是并没有。他一遍又一遍地看着,希望是自己看漏了,或者字母顺序排错了。那天他独自回家,进屋后便哭了。史密斯明白所发生的一切。迈克尔伤心的时候,不愿意见人。

兰尼的助理教练弗雷德·林奇后来说:"我们知道迈克尔很好,但我们想让他多练练,觉得二队更适合他。"那一年他很容易就成为二队中最出色的队员。凭借着敏捷而并非身高,他成为队中的主力。有些比赛他能得到四十分。事实上他的突出表现使二队的比赛相当受欢迎。为了能看到他参加的二队比赛,整个校队的队员都提早到场。

史密斯发现乔丹在落选之前不甘人后,而在落选之后他的好胜心似乎有过之而无不及,好像决心不让落选重演。他的教练们也注意到了这一点。罗恩·科利说:"当我第一次看到迈克尔·乔丹时,还不知道他是谁。我一直在帮助兰尼校运动队。我们去与劲敌高兹保罗队打比赛。我走进体育馆时,二队的比赛就要结束了。场上的其他九名队员都已无心恋战,只有一个孩子还在竭尽全力。看他打球的样子,我想他的队在剩下的两分钟里也就只落后了一分吧。可当我抬头看计时钟时,他们队竟落后有二十分,而比赛只剩下了最后一分钟。这就是迈克尔,我很快就知道了他一贯如此。”

他与以前一样努力,是队中最勤于练球的队员。如果发现队友不够努力,他会亲自说服他们,有时鼓动教练去说服。一时间兰尼中学有了一个非常优秀的篮球队,迈克尔·乔丹成了冉冉升起的明星。

Lance Armstrong: The Living Legend

Lance Armstrong the living legend in world of cycling was born on September 18, 1971. His parents got separated when he was young and he was raised by his mother. He took active part in the sport events. He got the Iron Kids Triathlon and became a professional athlete while he was just 16. Initially he was interested in swimming and running events of triathlon competition but later he left them. He was enthralled by cycling competition and decided to make a career in it. By the time he was in high school he had cycling sponsors ready to sponsor him.

Lance told to media that he was born to race bikes. This fact is evident from his school days naughty activities. He had such a craze for cycling that he would go out for short tours with his friends and many times he went so far that he had to ring up to his mother to pick him up. He got qualified to train with the U. S. Olympic developmental team in Colorado Springs, during his senior year of high school. The busy training schedule unfocused him totally from studies. He could have failed to qualify the exams of high school diploma, but during the final weeks of the school year he joined private tuitions, which enabled Lance to graduate on time. On completion of graduation he turned his attention totally towards cycling.

In 1989 Lance made himself eligible for the junior world championships. Lance got many new things to learn from the amateur competition. Not only was he rectified his cycling skills, but this experience exposed him to outside world. This played on his minds and brought a change in his behavior. He became brave and confident. By 1991, he became the U. S. National Amateur Champion.

He then participated in his first professional race in 1992 at Classico San Sebastian. He was not capable to perform to his standards. He finished the race 27 minutes after the winner. Anyone other at his place would have said a goodbye to the game.

From this experience he learnt many new things and rectified all his past mistakes to make himself perfect in all sense. He got 10 titles in 1993 which also included winning the U. S. PRO Championship and became the youngest road racing world champion. This was a result of all shear determination and approach even after his failure in San Sebastian Olympic Games. He also marked success with great notice as he became the first from U. S. team, Lance's Team Motorola, to be ranked among the top five in the world.

After challenging in the 1996 Olympics in Atlanta, Armstrong started to feel tired and weak and couldn't race as well as he used to. Doctors told Lance he had cancer in his testicles. His career would have finished that day were it not for the influence of his hard working mother, who remains his biggest hero even today. It was an inspiring experience that strengthened his resolves but set the tone for his career. He credits a lot to Bristol-Myers Squibb, who produced the drugs with which his cancer could be removed.

Lance Armstrong made a comeback to cycling in 1998 and in 1999 he entered the exhausting Tour de France, a 2, 274 mile race through the Alps. Armstrong capitalized his top position in the race from start to finish and won the event by nearly seven minutes. His astonishing comeback from cancer made him a world-wide celebrity and an inspiration for other people with cancer. He got the title of the Tour de France from 1999 to 2002 and won again in 2003 for a record-tying fifth consecutive title.

He has taken his success and transformed it into hope for all the individuals who face cancer every day. He has set up "The Lance Armstrong Foundation" to promote cancer research and awareness. He joined hands with Bristol-Myers Squibb to support early cancer detection; to reduce fear associated with cancer and to encourage a team approach to treatment.

He showed to world "whatever the mind can conceive and believe, the mind can achieve." The moral we get from him is that successful people don't do great things; they only do small things in a great way.

兰斯·阿姆斯特朗：活着的传奇

兰斯·阿姆斯特朗，是自行车世界里活着的传奇，他出生于1971年9月18日。在他还是个孩子的时候，父母就离婚了，他是由母亲抚养长大的。兰斯·阿姆斯特朗乐于参加各种体育活动，他曾获得少年组铁人三项赛的桂冠，并在16岁时成为了一名专业的铁人三项运动员。最初，他对三项赛中的游泳和赛跑很感兴趣,后来便转而被自行车项目所吸引,继而决定以此作为自己的事业。在兰斯·阿姆斯特朗上高中的时候,就有自行车赞助商来赞助他了。

兰斯曾对媒体表示他就是为自行车运动而生的。这一点从他学生时代淘气的表现中就可以证明。他痴迷于自行车运动,以至于在和朋友们作短程旅行的时候经常由于骑得太远而不得不让母亲开车来接他。在高中三年级的时候,他获得了到科罗拉多州和美国奥运预备队一起训练的机会。紧张的训练影响了他的学习,要不是在毕业前的几周里接受了私下的辅导,他差点毕不了业。高中毕业后,他就把全部的精力都投注在自行车运动上了。

1989 年,兰斯获得了参加世界少年自行车锦标赛的资格。在比赛中,他学到了许多新事情。他不但改进了自己的自行车技艺,还对外面的世界有了进一步的了解。经历了这些之后,兰斯在思想和行为上都产生了变化,他变得更加自信和勇敢。1991 年他成为美国业余锦标赛的冠军。

1992 年兰斯第一次参加了在塞巴斯地安举行的职业自行车比赛即奥运会自行车赛。最终他以落后冠军 27 分钟的成绩完成了比赛。要是换了其他人,面对这样的成绩肯定就会对这项运动说再见了。

然而兰斯从这次经历中又学到了许多,他改进了过去的一些错误,使自己在各方面更加完美。1993 年他获得了包括美国自行车公开赛的10项冠军头衔并成为最年轻的公路赛世界冠军。这一切都源于他坚毅的决心和1992年奥运会失败后付出的种种努力。兰斯的成功使他成为美国摩托罗拉车队历史上第一个排名世界前五的车手。

参加完1996年亚特兰大奥运会后，兰斯开始感到疲惫和虚弱，他不再能像以往那样去比赛了。医生诊断兰斯患上了睾丸癌。要不是受到意志坚强的母亲的影响，兰斯的职业生涯从那时起就会结束，直到今天，母亲仍是兰斯心目中最大的英雄。兰斯下定决心要战胜癌症。他充分信任布里斯托尔医生能够研制出治愈他疾病的药。

1998年兰斯重新回到他所热爱的自行车运动中来。1999年他参加了漫长的环法自行车赛，选手们要骑车穿越阿尔卑斯山，赛程2 274英里。比赛中，阿姆斯特朗从始至终处于领先地位，最后以领先第二名大约7分钟的成绩获得胜利。他的这次战胜癌症的经历令世人震惊，使他成为名人，对其他癌症患者也是一个巨大的鼓舞。从1999年到2003年中，他创纪录地连续五次获得环法自行车赛的冠军。

他把他的成功转化为对所有其他癌症病人的鼓舞和希望。他创立了"阿姆斯特朗基金会"来促进对癌症的研究和发现。他和布里斯托尔医生一起为癌症的尽早发现而努力，减少人们对癌症的恐惧，并且鼓励在癌症治疗方面的合作。

阿姆斯特朗通过自己的行动告诉世人：只要你有希望和梦想，就可以实现它们。从他的身上，我们看到，成功的人不一定要去做伟大的事情，而是以伟大的方式去做一些小事。

后　　记

本书英文材料大多选自国外报刊。有些篇目采用的是现存译文,因一时无法找到译者,故未及商谈著作权事宜,甚为抱歉。望译者见本书后与我们联系,以便及时奉上薄酬。

图书在版编目（CIP）数据

英汉对照名人故事 / 逸云选编. -- 上海 : 文汇出版社, 2014.10

ISBN 978-7-5496-1288-8

Ⅰ.①英… Ⅱ.①逸… Ⅲ.①英语－汉语－对照读物②名人－生平事迹－世界 Ⅳ.①H319.4：K

中国版本图书馆CIP数据核字(2014)第221896号

英汉对照名人故事

选　　编 / 逸　云

责任编辑 / 陈今夫
特约编辑 / 文　荣
装帧设计 / 张　晋

出版发行 / 文匯出版社
上海市威海路755号
（邮政编码200041）
经　　销 / 全国新华书店
印刷装订 / 江苏省启东市人民印刷有限公司
版　　次 / 2014年10月第1版
印　　次 / 2014年10月第1次印刷
开　　本 / 850×1168 1 / 32
字　　数 / 120千字
印　　张 / 7.875

书　　号 / 978-7-5496-1288-8
定　　价 / 20.00元

《英汉对照幽默集萃》

逸云选编　定价: 15 元

Overcrowded Moon

A geography teacher once told her class, "The moon is so large that several million people could live there."

One boy started laughing, "It sure must get crowded when it's a crescent moon."

拥挤的月亮

一位地理老师告诉他的学生:"月亮非常大,可以容纳几百万人在上面居住。"

有个男孩笑了,"当月亮由满月变成月牙时,住在上面的人一定很拥挤。"

《英汉对照名人名言》

刘文荣选编　定价: 18 元

If the only tool you have is a hammer, you tend to see every problem as a nail.

[America] Abraham Maslow

如果你唯一的工具是一把锤子,你往往会把一切问题都看成钉子。

[美国]亚伯拉罕·马斯洛